SWEDISH WITH PURPOSE

Come Play. In Swedish.

Mark Anderson, PhD

Säg något på svenska.

SWEDISH WITH PURPOSE: ***Come Play. In Swedish.***

Mark Anderson, PhD

Säg något på svenska. | Say Something in Swedish.

Copyright

Cover Images: Artwork was generated with artificial intelligence as a tool. The front cover image depicts Stockholm at blue hour, Sweden. The back cover image is of a generated Swedish Darla horse. Any resemblance to actual scenes is coincidental.

First Edition
Printed in the United States of America

ISBN: 979-8-9958085-5-8 (ebook)
ISBN: 979-8-9958085-6-5 (paperback)

Disclaimer

This book is intended for educational and personal language-learning purposes only. It does not provide legal, medical, psychological, or professional advice.

Every effort has been made to ensure accuracy and clarity; however, language learning is an ongoing process, and readers are encouraged to use multiple resources as they develop skills and fluency.

All sample dialogues, scenarios, and conversation engines are fictional and not based on real individuals unless explicitly stated. Any resemblance to actual persons, living or dead, is coincidental.

The author and publisher assume no responsibility for errors or outcomes resulting from the use of the methods, patterns, or examples in this book. Use wisely, practice freely, and adapt creatively. The book can function as a dual-direction language platform.

Dedication

For every learner who ever sat with a cup of coffee, opened a book, and began a journey into another world.

Acknowledgments

My heartfelt thanks to my sister, whose encouragement and curiosity have been the wind behind these pages. She reminded me that ideas grow when shared with someone who truly cares.

To my friends and the kind people I've met along the way — thank you for the conversations in cafés, train stations, and in between moments. They remind me that every language begins with connection.

And finally, to you — the readers, teachers, and learners — thank you for joining this journey. The greatest adventure is understanding one another in every language.

Adventure in Every Language.

Table of Contents

Copyright....2
Disclaimer....2
Dedication....2
Acknowledgments....3
Table of Contents....4
Publisher's Note....15
Preface....17
Brief Pronunciation Guide....18
Conversation Starters....19
Starter Example....24
How to Use This Book....25
Engine 1: Greetings & Opening Connection....28
Engine 2: Everyday Feelings & "How Are You Really?"....28
Engine 3: Weather & Everyday Observations....29
Engine 4: Plans, Intentions & "What Are You Up To?"....29
Engine 5: How Was Your Weekend?....30
Engine 6: What Are Your Plans for the Weekend?....30
Engine 7: How's Your Morning Going?....31
Engine 8: What's Happening Today?....31
Engine 9: Busy? Tired? Energized?....32
Engine 10: Any News Today?....32
Engine 11: Something Small I Noticed....33
Engine 12: Compliments & Positive Noticing....33
Engine 13: Coffee Small Talk....34
Engine 14: Work - Study - Daily Grind Check-In....34
Engine 15: Traffic, Commuting & Getting Here....35
Engine 16: Sleep & Rest Small Talk....36
Engine 17: How's everything with you?....36
Engine 18: Shared Environment Small Talk....37

Engine 19: What Are You Into Lately? 37
Engine 20: What You're Working on Lately....38
Engine 21: What do you think of…? 38
Engine 22: Do you recommend…? 39
Engine 23: Asking for Help (Light, Everyday Requests) 39
Engine 24: Offering Help (Light, Friendly Assistance)....40
Engine 25: Sharing Something Funny with Humor 40
Engine 26: Sharing a Small Challenge or Annoyance....41
Engine 27: Something You're Looking Forward To....41
Engine 28: Something New You Learned....42
Engine 29: Something You're Curious About....42
Engine 30: A Small Comfort or Treat You Enjoy....43
Engine 31: Sharing Something You Noticed....43
Engine 32: A Small Decision You Made Today....44
Engine 33: A Question You've Been Meaning to Ask....44
Engine 34: Sharing a Tiny Achievement 45
Engine 35: Something You've Been Avoiding....46
Engine 36: A Small Joy or Surprise in Your Day....46
Engine 37: Something You're Thinking About Changing....47
Engine 38: Planning Something in the Near Future....47
Engine 39: Something You Appreciated Today....48
Engine 40: Something You're Curious to Try 49
Engine 41: A Memory That Came to Mind 49
Engine 42: Something Positive Noticed About Someone Else....50
Engine 43: Something You're Grateful For....50
Engine 44: Something That Caught Your Eye 51
Engine 45: A Small Preference You Have 52
Engine 46: Something You're Looking Forward To 52
Engine 47: Something That Recently Inspired You 53
Engine 48: A Question You've Been Thinking About 53
Engine 49: Something You Recently Learned....54

Engine 50: A Small Improvement You Made Recently.....55
Engine 52: A Small Habit You're Working On.....56
Engine 53: A Routine You Enjoy.....57
Engine 54: Noticing Something Interesting About People.....57
Engine 55: Something That Made You Smile Recently.....58
Engine 56: A Nice View or Visual Moment You Noticed.....58
Engine 57: Something That Surprised You In a Good Way.....59
Engine 58: Something You Changed Your Mind About.....60
Engine 59: Something You Realized About Yourself.....60
Engine 60: Something You're Hoping For.....61
Engine 61: Something That Motivates You Lately.....61
Engine 62: Something You Handled Better Than Expected.....62
Engine 63: Something You Want to Get Better At.....63
Engine 64: Something You Don't Enjoy, But May Need to Do.....63
Engine 65: Something That Frustrated You Briefly But You Got Over It.....64
Engine 66: Something That Made You Smile Today.....64
Engine 67: Something You Appreciated Today.....65
Engine 68: Something You Noticed Today - Observation, Not Opinion.....66
Engine 69: Something You Wondered About Today.....66
Engine 70: Something You Found Interesting Recently.....67
Engine 71: Something You Would Recommend to Someone.....68
Engine 72: Something You've Been Enjoying Lately.....68
Engine 73: Something You'd Like to Try Soon.....69
Engine 74: Something You Prefer (But Don't Always Get).....70
Engine 75: Something You Usually Choose Between Two Options.....70
Engine 76: Something You Do Almost Every Day (But Isn't a "Habit" Yet).....71
Engine 77: Something You Don't Do Often, But Enjoy Every Time.....71
Engine 78: Something That Comforts You.....72
Engine 79: Something You Love the Sound Of.....73
Engine 80: Something You Love the Look Of.....73
Engine 81: Something You Love the Smell Of.....74

Engine 82: Something You Like the Feel Of (Sensation)..75
Engine 83: A Temperature or Weather Feeling You Really Enjoy..........................75
Engine 84: A Kind of Light You Love (Morning, Evening, Indoors, Night)........76
Engine 85: A Time of Day You Really Enjoy..76
Engine 86: A Day of the Week That Feels Good to You and Why........................77
Engine 87: A Season or Month That Feels Special to You.......................................78
Engine 88: A Place (Big or Small) That Makes You Feel Calm...............................78
Engine 89: Something You Enjoy Doing With Other People.................................79
Engine 90: A Type of Conversation You Find Easy..80
Engine 91: A Type of Conversation You Find Challenging.....................................80
Engine 92: Something You Appreciate in a Friend...81
Engine 93: Something You Notice in People Quickly...82
Engine 94: How You Usually Introduce Yourself...82
Engine 95: A Cultural Habit You Find Interesting...83
Engine 96: How You Like to Plan Your Week...84
Engine 97: A Habit You Want to Build or Improve...84
Engine 98: A Piece of Advice You Often Give Others..85
Engine 99: A Small Dream You Hope to Fulfill Someday...86
Engine 100: Something That Helps You Feel Grounded..86
Engine 101: How You Recharge After a Busy Day..87
Engine 102: A Quality You Are Working to Strengthen in Yourself......................88
Engine 103: A Sign That You Feel Comfortable With Someone............................89
Engine 104: A Routine That Makes Your Mornings Better......................................89
Engine 105: A Value You Try to Live By..90
Engine 106: Something You Admire in Other People...90
Engine 107: Something You've Learned About Yourself...91
Engine 108: Something New You Want to Learn This Year....................................92
Engine 109: A Way You Like to Encourage Other People..92
Engine 110: A Sound That Makes You Feel Relaxed..93
Engine 111: A Lesson You Learned the Hard Way...94
Engine 112: A Small Joy From Your Week..94

Engine 113: Something You Value in a Friendship....95
Engine 114: A Goal You Want to Focus on This Month....95
Engine 115: Something From Your Culture That You're Proud Of....96
Engine 116: A Symbol That Represents You Right Now....97
Engine 117: Something That Motivates You When You Feel Low....97
Engine 118: A Place Where You Feel Completely Safe....98
Engine 119: A Quality You Appreciate in Other People....99
Engine 120: Something That Helps You Reset After a Stressful Day....100
Engine 121: A Habit You Want to Build Into Your Life....100
Engine 122: A Memory That Always Makes You Smile....101
Engine 123: Something You Hope to Experience in the Next Few Years....102
Engine 124: A Decision That Changed You for the Better....102
Engine 125: A Feeling You Wish You Could Hold Onto Longer....103
Engine 126: A Path You Might Have Taken in Another Version of Your Life..104
Engine 127: Advice You Would Give to Your Younger Self....104
Engine 128: A Moment When You Surprised Yourself....105
Engine 129: A Sensation or Sound That Brings You Calm....106
Engine 130: Something You've Learned to Appreciate More with Time....106
Engine 131: A Small Act of Kindness You'll Never Forget....107
Engine 132: Something You Consider a Personal Strength - That You Didn't Notice at First....108
Engine 133: Something You Look Forward to in the Next Chapter of Your Life....108
Engine 134: A Lesson You Learned the Hard Way But Are Grateful For Now 109
Engine 135: A Small Daily Ritual That Makes Your Day Better....110
Engine 136: Something Small That Always Makes You Smile....110
Engine 137: Something You Believe Is Worth Protecting....111
Engine 138: Something You Didn't Think You Could Do, But Eventually Did 112
Engine 139: A Memory That Still Feels Vivid, Even After Many Years....113
Engine 140: A Version of Yourself You're Growing Into....113
Engine 141: A Quality You Deeply Appreciate in Others....114

Engine 142: A Priority That Has Become Clearer to You Over Time.................115
Engine 143: A Gesture That Made You Feel Truly Understood...........................115
Engine 144: A Way You See Yourself Differently Now Than Before.................116
Engine 145: A Boundary You've Learned to Set..117
Engine 146: A Moment When You Were Braver Than You Realized.................117
Engine 147: Someone Who Helped You Grow in an Unexpected Way 118
Engine 148: Something You Wish You Had Realized Earlier in Life..................119
Engine 149: Something You Haven't Done Yet but Still Want to Do 119
Engine 150: A Lesson Life Keeps Teaching You Again and Again......................120
Engine 151: Gently Steering a Conversation Back on Course...............................121
Engine 152: Finding Common Ground Through Humor......................................122
Engine 153: Repairing a Misstep with Grace and Humor......................................122
Engine 154: Redirecting the Conversation Without Creating Friction 123
Engine 155: Pausing with Confidence Before Moving Forward...........................124
Engine 156: Naming the Direction of the Conversation..124
Engine 157: Summarizing Meaning Before Moving On 125
Engine 158: Staying with Ambiguity Without Forcing an Answer.......................126
Engine 159: Disagreeing Without Creating Opposition..126
Engine 160: Setting a Clear Boundary While Staying Warm.................................127
Engine 161: Reframing a Situation Without Dismissing Feelings..........................128
Engine 162: Letting Silence Create Space for the Other Person...........................128
Engine 163: Asking the Question That Changes the Frame..................................129
Engine 164: Accepting What You Can't Control 129
Engine 165: Choosing Meaning Even When Outcomes Are Uncertain...............130
Engine 166: Acting with Integrity When No One Is Watching............................131
Engine 167: Letting Go of Being Right to Stay Truthful 131
Engine 168: Choosing Silence as a Conscious Response 132
Engine 169: Knowing When a Conversation Has Done Its Work........................133
Engine 170: Choosing the Next Step Without Urgency...133
Engine 171: Acting Without Needing Recognition...134
Engine 172: Remaining Steady When Results Are Delayed...................................134

Engine 173: Staying Aligned When Motivation Fades....135
Engine 174: Choosing Consistency Over Intensity....135
Engine 175: Continuing When No One Is Watching Anymore....136
Engine 176: Remaining Open to Learning Even After Mastery....137
Engine 177: Releasing Certainty to Stay Adaptable....137
Engine 178: Choosing Clarity Over Comfort....138
Engine 179: Standing by a Decision Even When It's Uncomfortable....138
Engine 180: Accepting Trade-offs Without Regret....139
Engine 181: Holding Responsibility Without Self-Judgment....140
Engine 182: Letting Go of Control While Staying Responsible....140
Engine 183: Staying Grounded When Others Project Expectations Onto You....141
Engine 184: Saying No Without Guilt....141
Engine 185: Ending a Role or Chapter Without Bitterness....142
Engine 186: Beginning Again Without Discarding the Past....143
Engine 187: Holding Hope Without Illusion....143
Engine 188: Choosing Peace Over Being Right....144
Engine 189: Accepting Ambiguity Without Anxiety....144
Engine 190: Living With Integrity When No Rulebook Applies....145
Engine 191: Choosing Meaning Over Ease....146
Engine 192: Staying Kind Without Being Naïve....146
Engine 193: Acting With Courage Even When Fear Remains....147
Engine 194: Letting Success Change You Without Losing Yourself....147
Engine 195: Handling Influence Responsibly....148
Engine 196: Staying Curious Rather Than Cynical....149
Engine 197: Listening More Than Speaking....149
Engine 198: Knowing When to Speak....150
Engine 199: Letting Silence Speak....150
Engine 200: Ending Without Closure....151
Engine 201: Recognizing Meaning Patterns....151
Engine 202: Verbmönster du redan använder....160
Engine 203: Vardagsnyheter & gemensam verklighet....166

Engine 204: Travel & Mobility 168
Engine 205: Doctor Visit Regarding Health & Symptoms 169
Engine 206: Talking to Police for Safety & Directions 169
Engine 207: Ordering Coffee & Café Life 170
Engine 208: Ordering Breakfast, Lunch or Dinner 170
Engine 209: Ordering on the Phone - Pizza / Delivery 171
Engine 210: Asking for Directions 171
Engine 211: Airport & Flying 172
Engine 212: Shopping & Services in a Store 172
Engine 213: Grocery Store & Services 173
Engine 214: Meeting New People, Social Life & Relationships 173
Engine 215: Bank / Payment Issue 174
Engine 216: Emergency Call or Critical Situation 174
Engine 217: Pharmacy, Health & Medicine 175
Engine 218: Making Social Life Plans 175
Engine 219: Buying Public Transportation, Tickets, Travel 176
Engine 220: Housing / Landlord 176
Engine 221: Post Office / Package Pickup 177
Engine 222: Restaurant Problem 177
Engine 223: Taxi Ride 177
Engine 224: Hairdresser or Barber 178
Engine 225: Visiting Someone's Home 178
Engine 226: Small Talk at Work 178
Engine 227: Phone or Internet Service 179
Engine 228: Job Interview 179
Engine 229: First Day at Work 180
Engine 230: School, University or Education 180
Engine 231: Gym and Fitness 180
Engine 232: Hobby Course 181
Engine 233: Customer Service and Complaint 181
Engine 234: Childcare School Parent Talk 181

Engine 235: Making a Phone Appointment 182
Engine 236: Talking About the Weather 182
Engine 237: Holidays & Celebrations 182
Engine 238: Invitations & Events 183
Engine 239: Technology Help 183
Engine 240: Saying Goodbye and Moving Away 183
Engine 241: Gas Station and Fuel 184
Engine 242: Car Repair and Mechanic 184
Engine 243: Government Office Registration 185
Engine 244: Hospital Visiting Someone 185
Engine 245: Online Order and Returning a Package 186
Engine 246: Time, Dates & Numbers Overview 186
Engine 247: How Was Your Evening? 188
Engine 248: I Broke My Leg Skiing 189
Engine 249: Reporting an Incident to Police 190
Engine 250: Being Questioned as a Witness 191
Engine 251: Traffic Stop Explanation 191
Engine 252: Filing a Formal Written Statement 192
Engine 253: Explaining an Accident with Another Driver 193
Engine 254: Asking About Legal Rights Politely 193
Engine 255: Choosing a Major or Field of Study 194
Engine 256: Discussing a Challenging Class 194
Engine 257: Debating an Academic Idea 195
Engine 258: Applying for a Research Position 196
Engine 259: Presenting a Thesis Topic 197
Engine 260: Challenging a Professor Respectfully 197
Engine 261: Defending an Argument in a Seminar 198
Engine 262: Discussing AI and Ethics 199
Engine 263: Negotiating Respectfully 199
Engine 264: Giving Constructive Feedback 200
Engine 265: Cross-Cultural Discussion 200

Engine 266: Conflict De-Escalation 201
Engine 267: Human–AI Responsibility Conversation 202
Engine 268: Continuing the Conversation 202
Engine 269: Natural Conversation Fillers 203
Engine 270: Listener Responses 205
Engine 271: Thinking Words 206
Engine 272: Softening Your Opinion 207
Engine 273: Agreeing and Disagreeing Politely 208
Engine 274: Conversation Extenders 210
Engine 275: Essential Everyday Phrases 211
Engine 276: Starter, Follow-up, Deepen, Close Builder 214
Starter (Reflektio) 215
Starter (Expansion) 218
Follow-Up 222
Follow-Up (Expansion) 224
Deepen (Reflection / Insight Layer) 227
Deepen (Expansion) 231
Close (Wrap-Up Engine) 234
Close (Expansion) 238
Engine 277: Standardsvenska vs vardagligt tal 241
Engine 278: Vardagliga verkliga samtal 243
Engine 279: Try Other Languages 245
Engine 280: The Conversation Toolkit 249
Engine 281: Flea Circus 251
Engine 282: Good Study Habits 253
Engine 283: Selective Word Substitutions 254
Engine 284: Talking about Emotions 256
Engine 285: Descriptions 256
Engine 286: Simple Introductions 258
Engine 287: The Conversation Continues 259

Appendix 1: Quick Guide: "en" and "ett" Nouns....261
Appendix 2: Pronunciation Guide....263
Appendix 3: Swedish Sound Quick Map....268
Appendix 4: Top 20 Swedish Pronunciation Fixes....270
Author's Intent....277
About the Author....278
Back Cover....279
Description....279
How the Engines were designed....280
Also by Mark Anderson....283
Selected References....283

Publisher's Note

The brain is efficient.
We remember what we actively use.

Most language books begin with rules.
Grammar tables. Vocabulary lists. Explanations. Powerful indeed.
These are important — but, we also need core communication skills. Then we can enthusiastically exploit pattern recognition and grammar rules.

This book begins with conversation.

Language is learned through patterns, practice, and wonderful human interaction. Instead of memorizing isolated words first, *Swedish with Purpose* introduces small, reusable **conversation engines** — compact dialogues that reflect real situations in daily life.

Work through the conversation engines aloud — with repetition, focus, and intention — and something begins to change.

Conversation no longer feels distant. It becomes usable.

With consistent practice, learners can build toward B1-level speaking, move into B2 in everyday situations, and even stretch toward C1-level performance in more demanding conversational tasks.

Each engine follows a simple rhythm:

Starter → Follow-Up → Deepen → Close

These patterns mirror how people naturally communicate and how the brain learns language through repetition and variation. By encountering the same conversational structures in different contexts, learners gradually build familiarity and confidence.

In the process, we seem to have created a small psychological progression:

1. **Invitation**
   Come play.

2. **Permission**
   Mistakes are fine. Correct as you learn.

3. **Simplicity**
   One word is enough.

4. **Action**
   Say Something in Swedish. Säg något på svenska.

That sequence lowers the fear barrier, which is what often stops people from speaking. Use "Säg något på svenska." as an easy icebreaker.

The tone of this book is intentionally relaxed. Conversation is not a test. It is a social activity. Readers are encouraged to read aloud, experiment with the phrases, and speak even when the words feel imperfect.

This is important because language is dynamic. These engines are only a starting point. At the end of this book, you are encouraged to build your own conversation engines. Mistakes and differences happen, but this helps us learn.

Practice with purpose.

More importantly, this approach builds something deeper: confidence, responsiveness, and the ability to think and speak in the moment.

Because when we practice with purpose, we do more than memorize words — we begin to think, respond, and take part in real conversations in Swedish.

Talk with a friend — or your favorite coffee cup.

Yes. Really. Come play.

If this book helps you say **even one sentence in Swedish**,
the conversation has already begun.

Preface

Swedish with Purpose

Come Play. In Swedish.

This book is designed to help us practice in a way that is active, intentional, and immediately connected to real communication.

Language is one of humanity's oldest technologies. Long before machines learned to speak, people shaped the world through questions, stories, and conversation. Stories are shared using the vocabulary we know.

Children do not learn language by studying grammar charts first. They learn by hearing patterns, repeating them, and using them with purpose. Conversation teaches us how language actually works. Then grammar.

Fluency does not grow from random vocabulary lists.
It grows from repetition, rhythm, and meaningful interaction.

This book begins speaking from day one.

Instead of scattered phrases, you will find short, reusable **conversation engines** — compact dialogues designed to mirror real interactions in daily life. Each engine has a clear purpose: greeting someone, sharing news, asking for help, expressing emotion, navigating uncertainty, and closing conversations naturally.

The idea began as a simple experiment:

Could small, reusable conversation frameworks help people speak sooner — and with more confidence?

The answer was yes.

These engines follow the pattern our brains already use:

Example → Recognition → Variation

We see a pattern.
We repeat it.
We adapt it.

Fluency accelerates.

Purpose is often the missing ingredient in language tools. Purpose turns repetition into progress and hesitation into action. These engines are not scripts or drills. They are structured conversations that move naturally through a simple sequence:

Starter → Follow-Up → Deepen → Close

This Swedish–English edition introduces conversational patterns helping us recognize how real conversations actually sound.

This book sits at the intersection of language learning, conversational design, and modern AI thinking — but it is written for people. Conversation is not just functional. It is social, curious, and sometimes delightfully imperfect.

This edition is a beginning. The framework is designed to grow across languages and cultures, helping us navigate conversations with confidence.

In short, this book explores the mechanics of dialogue —
and how to use them with purpose.

If you already have a method, teacher, tutor, or books that work for you, wonderful. These engines are a fun starting point. The book is designed to easily progress from one engine to the next, promoting dialog.

If you would like a book you can take with you and use with a friend over coffee, breakfast, lunch, or dinner, bring this one along.

Säg något på svenska. | Say Something in Swedish.

Brief Pronunciation Guide

(Say it out loud — perfection not required)

1. Swedish pronunciation is mostly consistent, but not perfectly phonetic. Some letters change sound depending on their position and surrounding letters.
2. Swedish vowels can be **short or long**, and this difference changes meaning. Common vowels include: a, e, i, o, u, y, å, ä, ö.
3. Long vowels are usually followed by a single consonant, while short vowels are often followed by double consonants (e.g., tak vs. tack).
4. Some consonants change sound depending on nearby vowels. For example, **k, g, and sk** can have "soft" or "hard" sounds.
5. The letters **sj, sk, stj, and skj** can produce a special "sh-like" sound that varies slightly by region.
6. Stress is usually placed on the **first syllable** of a word.
7. Swedish has a natural rhythm and melody — focus on the flow, not just individual sounds.

Conversation Starters

Säg något på svenska is more than a tagline. It is a starting point, an icebreaker. If you do not know where to start then start by saying "Säg något på svenska"! Use it as an icebreaker that encourages you to speak aloud.

Swedish - Svenska	English - Engelska
1. Greetings & Social Openings	
Hej	Hello / Hi
God morgon	Good morning
God eftermiddag	Good afternoon
God kväll	Good evening
Hur mår du?	How are you?
Jag mår bra	I'm fine
Trevligt att träffas	Nice to meet you
Välkommen	Welcome
2. Introductions & Identity	
Jag heter…	My name is…
Vad heter du?	What is your name?
Jag kommer från…	I am from…
Var kommer du ifrån?	Where are you from?
Jag bor i…	I live in…
Jag är student / lärare / ingenjör	I am a student / teacher / engineer
3. Basic Questions	
Vad är det här?	What is this?
Vem är det där?	Who is that?
Var är …?	Where is…?
När börjar det?	When does it start?
Varför?	Why?
Hur?	How?
4. Directions & Location	
Var är toaletten?	Where is the bathroom?
Hur kommer jag till …?	How do I get to…?

Är det långt?	Is it far?
Sväng vänster / höger	Turn left / right
Gå rakt fram	Go straight
Det är nära / långt bort	It's near / far
5. Food & Ordering	
Jag skulle vilja ha…	I would like…
Kan jag få…?	Can I have…?
Menyn, tack	The menu, please
Vatten, tack	Water, please
Notan, tack	The bill, please
Det var gott	It was delicious
6. Shopping & Money	
Hur mycket kostar det här?	How much is this?
Det är för dyrt	That's too expensive
Har ni den här i en annan storlek?	Do you have this in another size?
Jag tar den	I'll take it
Kan jag betala med kort?	Can I pay by card?
7. Time & Scheduling	
Vad är klockan?	What time is it?
Idag / imorgon / igår	Today / tomorrow / yesterday
Nu / senare	Now / later
Jag är upptagen	I am busy
Vi ses …	Let's meet at…
Vi ses senare	See you later
8. Agreement & Opinions	
Ja / nej	Yes / No
Kanske	Maybe
Jag tror det	I think so
Jag håller med / jag håller inte med	I agree / disagree
Det är bra / dåligt	That's good / bad
Jag gillar det / jag gillar det inte	I like it / I don't like it
9. Help & Emergencies	

Hjälp!	Help!
Jag behöver hjälp	I need help
Ring polisen	Call the police
Jag har gått vilse	I am lost
Jag förstår inte	I don't understand
Kan du upprepa?	Can you repeat that?
10. Clarification & Conversation Control	
Tala långsammare, tack	Please speak slowly
Vad betyder det här?	What does this mean?
Hur säger man…?	How do you say…?
Kan du upprepa?	Can you repeat?
Jag lär mig svenska	I'm learning Swedish
11. Politeness & Social Norms	
Varsågod	Please / You're welcome
Tack	Thank you
Ursäkta	Excuse me / Sorry
12. Everyday Actions (Verb Core)	
Jag vill	I want
Jag behöver	I need
Jag går	I go
Jag kommer	I come
Jag äter	I eat
Jag arbetar	I work
Jag studerar	I study
13. People & Relationships	
Det här är min mamma / pappa / vän	This is my mother / father / friend
Har du syskon?	Do you have siblings?
Min vän bor i…	My friend lives in…
14. Daily Life & Routines	
Jag vaknar klockan…	I wake up at…
Jag går till jobbet	I go to work

Jag äter frukost	I eat breakfast
Jag tittar på TV	I watch TV
Jag går och lägger mig	I go to sleep

15. Descriptions (Adjectives & Properties)

Stor / liten	Big / small
Bra / dålig	Good / bad
Varm / kall	Hot / cold
Ny / gammal	New / old
Snabb / långsam	Fast / slow

16. Numbers, Quantity & Counting

Ett, två, tre…	One, two, three…
Hur många?	How many?
Mycket / lite	A lot / a little
Mer / mindre	More / less

17. RGB Colors

Röd	Red
Blå	Blue
Grön	Green

18. Prepositions & Spatial Concepts

I / på / under	In / on / under
Bredvid / mellan	Next to / between
Inne / ute	Inside / outside

19. Basic Grammar Structures

Jag är…	I am…
Du är…	You are…
Det här är…	This is…
Det finns…	There is…

20. Negation

Jag förstår inte	I don't understand
Jag vill inte	I don't want
Det finns inte	There is no…
Inte nu	Not now

21. Verb Conjugation Basics

Jag går	I go
Du går	You go
Han/hon går	He/she goes
Jag gick	I went
Jag ska gå	I will go

22. Simple Conversation Connectors

Och	And
Men	But
För att	Because
Så	So

23. Feelings & States

Jag är trött	I am tired
Jag är glad	I am happy
Jag är sjuk	I am sick
Jag känner mig bra / dålig	I feel good / bad

24. Transportation

Buss / tåg / taxi	Bus / train / taxi
Jag tar bussen	I take the bus
Var är stationen?	Where is the station?

25. Travel & Accommodation

Hotell	Hotel
Jag har en bokning	I have a reservation
En natt / två nätter	One night / two nights

26. Health & Basic Needs

Jag behöver en läkare	I need a doctor
Jag är sjuk	I am sick
Det gör ont här	It hurts here

27. Communication

Telefon	Phone
Meddelande	Message
E-post	Email

Jag ringer	I call
28. Intentions & Plans	
Jag vill gå	I want to go
Jag planerar att…	I plan to…
Jag ska…	I will…
Jag tänker…	I am going to…
29. Preferences & Choices	
Jag föredrar…	I prefer…
Det här är bättre	This is better
30. Common Set Phrases	
Självklart	Of course
Inga problem	No problem
Precis	That's right
Vänta lite	Wait a moment
z	
Jag vill + [sak]	I want + [object]
Jag behöver + [sak]	I need + [object]
32. Variation Within Familiarity	
Jag vill ha kaffe	I want coffee
Jag vill ha te	I want tea
Jag vill ha hjälp	I want help
33. Meta-Language	
Hur säger man…?	How do you say…?
Vad betyder det här?	What does this mean?
Jag lär mig svenska	I am learning Swedish

Starter Example

Start with "Hello", Follow-up, Deepen, then Close with "Goodbye"

Swedish - Svenska	**English - Engelska**
Hej! Hur mår du idag?	Hi! How's it going today?

Swedish - Svenska	**English - Engelska**
Ganska bra, tack. Och du?	Pretty well, thanks. What about with you?
Bra också! Vad heter du?	Good as well! What's your name?
Jag heter Matti. Vad heter du?	I'm Matti. What's your name?
Jag heter Tiina, trevligt att träffas!	I'm Tiina, nice to meet you!
Detsamma! Pratar du lite svenska förresten?	Likewise! Do you speak a bit of Swedish?
Lite grann, men jag övar varje dag.	A little, but I practice every day.
Vad bra! Hur gammal är du?	That's great! How old are you?
Jag är trettio. Och du?	I'm thirty. And you?
Jag är lite äldre. Ålder är bara en siffra.	I'm a little older. Age is just a number.
Det stämmer. Var kommer du ifrån?	True. Where are you from?
Jag kommer från USA, men jag bor nu i Stockholm.	I'm from the United States, but I live in Stockholm now.
Jaha, vad trevligt! Gillar du Stockholm?	Oh, nice! Do you like Stockholm?
Jag tycker mycket om det, det är vackert och lugnt.	I like it a lot, it's beautiful and calm.
Vad roligt att höra. Vi hörs snart igen!	Great to hear. Let's continue chatting soon!

How to Use This Book

For students, teachers, tutors — and maybe AI.

Conversation engines are **mini-lessons that teach themselves**.

They are only starting points. Mix and match to build larger conversations.

Average speech is about **120–150 words per minute**, so one engine takes about **a minute to read aloud**.

1. Say the lines aloud — then say them again.
2. Laugh at the mistakes — and keep going anyway.
3. Talk with a friend — or speak to your coffee cup.

Make the decision to play with Swedish.

Why this book?

Swedish with Purpose begins with a decision.
That decision begins conversations.
Conversations create familiarity.
Familiarity builds confidence.
Confidence is what we are building.

Talk with a friend — or your coffee cup.
Yes. Really. Come play.

Säg något på svenska.
Say something in Swedish.

Kom och lek. På svenska.
Come Play. In Swedish.

Ett ord räcker.
One word is enough.

Natural acquisition works. It has worked for millennia.
The question is not if it works —
the question is how to **accelerate it intentionally**.

It is **structured familiarity**.

If this book helps you say **even one sentence in Swedish,**
the conversation has already begun.

decision → conversation → familiarity → confidence → fun

Engine 1: Greetings & Opening Connection

Swedish - Svenska	English - Engelska
Hej! Hur har din dag börjat?	Hi! How has your day started?
Ganska bra, en lite hektisk morgon bara.	Pretty good, just a bit of a busy morning.
Jaha, hektisk? Vad hände?	Oh, busy? What happened?
Jag vaknade sent och allt gick i ett snabbt tempo.	I woke up late and everything felt rushed.
Jag förstår. Är det vanligt för dig?	I get it. Is that common for you?
Nja, ibland. Men idag kan jag redan skratta åt det.	Well, sometimes. But today I can laugh about it.
Vad bra att höra, tack för att du berättade.	Good to hear, thanks for sharing.
Vi fortsätter senare!	Let's continue later!

Engine 2: Everyday Feelings & "How Are You Really?"

Swedish - Svenska	English - Engelska
Hur mår du idag?	How are you doing today?
Lite trött, om jag ska vara ärlig.	A bit tired, honestly.
Jaha, trött? Vad beror det på?	Oh, tired? What caused that?
Jag sov dåligt och morgonen var hektisk.	I slept poorly and the morning was hectic.
Jag förstår. Hur kändes det egentligen för dig?	I get it. How did it really feel for you?
Ärligt talat, ganska tungt.	Honestly, kind of heavy.

Swedish - Svenska	English - Engelska
Tack för att du berättade, vi kan prata mer om det senare.	Thanks for sharing, we can talk more later.
Det låter bra.	Sounds good.

Engine 3: Weather & Everyday Observations

Swedish - Svenska	English - Engelska
Vilken vacker dag det är idag.	What a beautiful day it is today.
Verkligen, äntligen!	It really is, finally!
Ja, gillar du sånt här väder?	Yeah, do you like this kind of weather?
Ja, det ger mig direkt en bra känsla.	Yes, it always puts me in a good mood.
Vilken är din favoritårstid?	What's your favorite season?
Hösten. Jag gillar den svala luften och färgerna.	Autumn. I love the cool air and the colors.
Jag förstår, tack för att du berättade.	I understand, thanks for sharing.
Vi pratar mer senare.	Let's talk more later.

Engine 4: Plans, Intentions & "What Are You Up To?"

Vad tänker du göra idag?	What are you planning for today?
Jag funderar på att gå en sväng på stan.	I'm thinking of going into town.
Det låter trevligt, hur länge blir du borta?	Sounds nice, how long will that take?

Kanske bara ett par timmar.	Maybe just a couple of hours.
Är det något som är viktigt för dig?	Is this something important to you?
Nja, jag gillar bara att strosa runt och koppla av.	Well, I just enjoy wandering around and relaxing.
Det låter bra, njut av dagen.	Sounds good, enjoy your day.
Tack!	Thanks!

Engine 5: How Was Your Weekend?

Hur var din helg?	How was your weekend?
Riktigt bra, jag var ute och träffade en vän.	Really good, I went outside and met a friend.
Vad trevligt! Vad gjorde ni?	Nice! What did you two do?
Vi tog en lång promenad och tog en kaffe.	We took a long walk and had coffee.
Vad var helgens höjdpunkt?	What was the highlight of the weekend?
Nog stunden när solen kom fram.	Probably the moment when the sun came out.
Det låter härligt, vi pratar mer om det en annan gång.	Sounds lovely, let's talk more about it another time.
Absolut.	Definitely.

Engine 6: What Are Your Plans for the Weekend?

Har du några planer för helgen?	Do you have any plans for the weekend?
Ja, jag funderar på att åka till stugan.	Yes, I'm thinking of going to the cottage.

Åh vad trevligt! Vad tänker du göra där?	Oh nice! What do you plan to do there?
Mest ta det lugnt och kanske basta.	Mostly relax and maybe go to the sauna.
Härligt, vad gör en helg bra för dig?	Lovely, what makes a good weekend for you?
Att inte ha bråttom.	Just not having any rush.
Det låter perfekt, njut av helgen!	Sounds perfect, enjoy your weekend!
Tack, det ska jag!	Thanks, I will!

Engine 7: How's Your Morning Going?

Hur har din morgon varit?	How's your morning going?
Ganska bra, jag drack kaffe och läste lite nyheter.	Pretty well, had some coffee and read a bit of news.
Vad trevligt, hur kändes morgonen?	Nice, how did the morning feel to you?
Lugnt, vilket var väldigt skönt.	Calm, which was really nice.
Är det en typisk morgon för dig?	Is this a typical morning for you?
Inte alltid, men idag fungerade det bra.	Not always, but today it worked.
Vad bra, jag hoppas att dagen fortsätter lika bra.	Great, hope your day continues just as well.
Tack, detsamma!	Thanks, you too!

Engine 8: What's Happening Today?

Vad står på schemat idag?	What's on your schedule today?
En ganska vanlig dag, ett par möten och lite arbete.	Pretty normal, a couple of meetings and some work tasks.

Det låter rimligt, är något särskilt viktigt?	Sounds reasonable, is anything especially important?
Ett projekt behöver komma framåt.	One project needs to move forward.
Vad skulle göra dagen lyckad för dig?	What would make today successful for you?
Om jag får projektet i bra form.	If I get that project into good shape.
Vad bra, jag hoppas det går bra.	Great, I hope it goes well.
Tack, jag uppskattar det!	Thanks, I appreciate that!

Engine 9: Busy? Tired? Energized?

Känner du dig trött eller pigg idag?	Feeling tired or energized today?
Ganska trött, jag sov inte så bra.	Pretty tired, I didn't sleep very well.
Jag förstår, vad gjorde dig trött?	Oh, I see, what tired you out?
Jag var uppe för sent med ett projekt.	I stayed up too late working on a project.
Jag förstår. Vad skulle hjälpa dig att må bättre?	I get it. What would help you feel better?
Kanske mer kaffe och en lugn stund.	Probably more coffee and a quiet moment.
Tack för att du berättade, hoppas du får mer energi snart.	Thanks for sharing, hope your energy improves soon.
Tack, vi får hoppas det!	Thanks, let's hope so!

Engine 10: Any News Today?

Har det hänt något nytt idag?	Any news today?

Nja, bussen var sen igen.	Well, the bus was late again.
Jaså? Berätta mer!	Oh really? Tell me more!
Den kom tio minuter sent och alla sprang.	It came ten minutes late and everyone was running.
Oj, vad var det roligaste?	Wow, what was the funniest part?
Någon sprang efter den med en kaffekopp i handen.	Someone chased it with a coffee cup in hand.
Haha, jag kan se det framför mig, det piggade upp lite.	Ha, I can picture it, that brightened my moment.
Kul att höra, vi pratar mer senare.	Glad to hear that, let's talk more later.

Engine 11: Something Small I Noticed

Jag märkte att det var väldigt ljust ute i morse.	I noticed it was really bright outside this morning.
Det var det, nästan som vårkänsla.	It was, almost felt like spring.
Ja, verkligen! Vad var det som fångade din uppmärksamhet?	Oh true! What caught your attention about it?
Ljuset kom bara så plötsligt.	The light just appeared so suddenly.
Gjorde det dig på bättre humör?	Did it put you in a good mood?
Ja, även lite ljus hjälper alltid.	Yes, even a little light always helps.
Precis, det piggade verkligen upp stunden!	Exactly, that brightened the moment!
Samma här, tack!	Same here, thanks!

Engine 12: Compliments & Positive Noticing

Jag gillar din jacka, den ser riktigt bra ut.	I like your jacket, it looks great.
Tack! Jag köpte den förra veckan.	Thanks! I bought it last week.
Vad fint! Är det en ny stil för dig?	Oh nice! Is that a new style for you?
Kanske lite, jag ville prova något annorlunda.	Maybe a little, I wanted to try something different.
Känns det som du?	Does it feel like "you"?
Ja, faktiskt känns det så.	Yes, actually it does.
Vad bra, den passar dig verkligen.	Great, it really looks good.
Tack, jag uppskattar det!	Thanks, I appreciate that!

Engine 13: Coffee Small Talk

Vad dricker du just nu? Kaffe eller te?	What are you drinking right now? Coffee or tea?
Kaffe, jag provade en ny smak.	Coffee, I tried a new flavor.
Jaså! Är det något nytt du testar?	Oh! Is that something new you're trying?
Ja, någon vaniljkaffe. Ganska gott!	Yeah, some kind of vanilla coffee. Pretty good!
Föredrar du starkt eller milt kaffe?	Do you prefer strong or mild coffee?
Starkt, men ibland är det kul att prova något annat.	Strong, but sometimes it's nice to try something different.
Det låter gott, njut av din dryck!	Sounds delicious, enjoy your drink!
Tack, det ska jag!	Thanks, I will!

Engine 14: Work - Study - Daily Grind Check-In

Hur går jobbet idag?	How's work going today?
Ganska bra, jag behöver få klart en stor uppgift.	Pretty well, I need to finish one big task.
Det låter intressant, vad jobbar du med?	Oh, that sounds interesting, what are you working on?
Jag uppdaterar en rapport och gör några kontroller.	Updating a report and doing a few checks.
Vad gör den uppgiften viktig för dig?	What makes that task important for you?
Jag vill få den i bra skick innan imorgon.	I want it in good shape before tomorrow.
Det låter bra, lycka till idag!	Sounds good, good luck with the day!
Tack, jag uppskattar det!	Thanks, appreciate it!

Engine 15: Traffic, Commuting & Getting Here

Hur var resan hit idag?	How was your commute today?
Ganska långsam, trafiken stannade ett par gånger.	Pretty slow, traffic stopped a couple of times.
Oj! Tog det lång tid?	Oh wow! Did it take long?
Ungefär tio minuter längre än vanligt.	About ten minutes more than usual.
Är det vanligt för dina morgnar?	Is this typical for your mornings?
Tyvärr ganska ofta.	Unfortunately, pretty often.
Skönt att du kom fram, hoppas det går smidigare imorgon.	Glad you made it, hope tomorrow is easier.
Tack, det hoppas jag också!	Thanks, me too!

Engine 16: Sleep & Rest Small Talk

Sov du bra i natt?	Did you sleep well last night?
Inte så bra, jag vaknade ett par gånger.	Not really, I woke up a couple of times.
Jaså? Vad påverkade din sömn?	Oh really? What affected your sleep?
Jag vet inte, kanske var jag bara rastlös.	Not sure, maybe I was just restless.
Vad brukar hjälpa dig att sova bättre?	What usually helps you sleep better?
En lätt kvällspromenad, men jag tog ingen igår.	A light evening walk, but I didn't take one yesterday.
Tack för att du berättade, hoppas nästa natt blir bättre.	Thanks for sharing, hope tonight is better.
Vi får hoppas det, tack!	Let's hope so, thanks!

Engine 17: How's everything with you?

Hur är det annars?	How are things going otherwise?
Ganska bra, en rätt vanlig vecka.	Pretty well, a fairly normal week.
Det låter stabilt, har något varit extra trevligt?	Sounds steady, has anything been especially nice?
Ja, en lugn kväll hemma var riktigt skön.	Well, one quiet evening at home was really nice.
Har något litet gett dig glädje?	Has anything small brought you joy?
Att jag äntligen fick vila lite.	Just being able to finally rest.
Vad bra att höra, hoppas resten av veckan blir lika bra.	Great to hear, hope the rest of the week goes just as well.
Tack, vi får hoppas det!	Thanks, let's hope so!

Engine 18: Shared Environment Small Talk

Det är verkligen lugnt här idag.	It's really quiet here today.
Ja, nästan ovanligt tyst.	Yes, almost unusually quiet.
Ja, verkligen! Hur känns det för dig?	Oh true! How does that feel to you?
Ganska rogivande faktiskt.	Actually pretty calming.
Föredrar du lugna eller livliga miljöer?	Do you prefer quiet or busy environments?
Lugna, det är lättare att fokusera.	Quiet, it's easier to focus.
Bra observation, vi fortsätter snart.	Nice observation, let's continue again soon.
Absolut, vi hörs!	Absolutely, talk to you later!

Engine 19: What Are You Into Lately?

Har du fastnat för något nytt på sistone?	Are you into anything new lately?
Ja, jag har börjat lyssna på en ny podcast.	Yeah, I started listening to a new podcast.
Vad intressant, vad gillar du med den?	Oh interesting, what appeals to you about it?
Den är avslappnad och rolig, perfekt på morgonen.	It's relaxed and funny, perfect for mornings.
Vad ger den dig i vardagen?	What does it give you in daily life?
En liten stund att skratta och lära mig något.	A small moment to laugh and learn something.
Vad kul, kanske testar jag också.	Nice, maybe I'll try it too.

Gör det, den är kort och lätt att lyssna på.	You should, it's short and easy to listen to.

Engine 20: What You're Working on Lately

Har du något litet mål för den här veckan?	Do you have any small goals for this week?
Ja, jag vill organisera ett skåp hemma.	Yeah, I want to organize one cabinet at home.
Vad bra! Hur tänker du börja?	Oh nice! How are you planning to start it?
Jag börjar med en hylla så att det inte blir för mycket.	I'll start with just one shelf so it's not overwhelming.
Vad motiverar dig i det här?	What motivates you in this?
Det känns bra att få även små saker i ordning.	It feels good to get even one small thing sorted.
Det låter bra, berätta senare hur det gick.	Sounds good, tell me later how it went.
Det ska jag, tack!	I will, thanks!

Engine 21: What do you think of…?

Har du provat det där nya caféet?	Have you tried that new café?
Ja, jag var där igår.	Yes, I went there yesterday.
Vad intressant, vad gillade du med det?	Oh interesting, what did you like about it?
Det hade en väldigt lugn atmosfär.	It had a really calm atmosphere.
Är det oftast din stil?	Is that usually your style?

Ja, jag gillar lugna caféer.	Yes, I like quiet cafés.
Fin synpunkt, jag uppskattar den.	Nice perspective, I appreciate it.
Tack, det var en trevlig pratstund!	Thanks, that was a nice little chat!

Engine 22: Do you recommend…?

Har du något att rekommendera just nu?	Do you have anything to recommend right now?
Ja, jag hittade ett riktigt bra café i centrum.	Yes, I found a really good café downtown.
Vad intressant, vad gör det så bra?	Oh interesting, what makes it good?
Det har en lugn atmosfär och riktigt bra kaffe.	It has a calm atmosphere and excellent coffee.
Har du en favorittyp av café?	Do you have a go-to type of café?
Lugnt och mysigt, ett ställe där man kan koppla av.	Quiet and cozy, a place you can really relax in.
Tack för tipset, jag ska prova det!	Thanks for the recommendation, I'll try it!
Berätta vad du tyckte när du varit där!	Let me know what you think when you go!

Engine 23: Asking for Help (Light, Everyday Requests)

Skulle du kunna hjälpa mig en stund?	Could you help me for a moment?
Självklart, vad gäller det?	Sure, what is it?
Jag behöver bara en snabb koll på det här.	I just need a quick check on this.

Okej, vi tittar.	Okay, let's see.
Ser du något som jag kan ha missat?	Do you see anything I might've missed?
Ja, där är en liten detalj som kan justeras.	Yeah, there's a small part that could be fixed.
Tack så mycket för hjälpen!	Thanks so much for your help!
Ingen fara, jag hjälper gärna!	No problem, happy to help!

Engine 24: Offering Help (Light, Friendly Assistance)

Behöver du hjälp?	Do you need any help?
Kanske lite, det här tar längre tid än jag trodde.	Maybe a little, this is taking more time than I expected.
Jag kan titta på det här om du vill.	I can check this if you'd like.
Tack, det vore jättebra.	Thanks, that would be really nice.
Vad skulle hjälpa dig mest just nu?	What would help you the most right now?
Om du bara kan kolla på den här delen.	If you could just look at this part.
Kul att kunna hjälpa till.	Glad I could help.
Tack, det hjälpte mycket.	Thanks, that helped a lot!

Engine 25: Sharing Something Funny with Humor

Jag såg något roligt i morse.	I saw something funny this morning.
Jaså, vad hände?	Oh, what happened?
Någon sprang till bussen med en kaffekopp i handen och höll på att spilla, men räddade det i sista stund.	Someone ran for the bus holding a coffee cup and almost spilled it, but saved it just in time.

Vad var roligast med det?	What was the funniest part?
Den fokuserade minen, som om det var en olympisk gren.	The focused expression, like balancing coffee was an Olympic sport.
Tack, det där gjorde min dag!	Thanks, that brightened my day!
Varsågod, jag var tvungen att berätta!	You're welcome, I had to share it!

Engine 26: Sharing a Small Challenge or Annoyance

Jag hade en liten utmaning idag.	I had a small challenge today.
Jaså, vad hände?	Oh, what happened?
Jag missade bussen med bara någon sekund.	I missed the bus by literally one second.
Vad tråkigt, berätta mer.	That's unfortunate, but tell me more.
Nästa kom först efter femton minuter och jag hade redan bråttom.	The next one came 15 minutes later, and I was already in a hurry.
Tur att det bara var en liten sak.	Luckily it was just a small thing.
Ja, nu känns det redan lite roligt.	True, now it already feels funny.

Engine 27: Something You're Looking Forward To

Har du något du ser fram emot den här veckan?	Do you have anything you're looking forward to this week?
Ja, jag ska ta en kvällspromenad med en vän på torsdag.	Yes, I'm going for an evening walk with a friend on Thursday.
Det låter trevligt, varför ser du fram emot det?	Oh, that sounds nice, why are you looking forward to it?

Det är alltid avkopplande och ett bra tillfälle att prata.	It's always relaxing and a great way to talk.
Är det ditt sätt att koppla av?	Is this your way to relax?
Ja, det nollställer dagen.	Yes, it resets the day.
Vad härligt att ha något att se fram emot.	So nice that you have something coming up.
Tack! Jag ser verkligen fram emot det.	Thanks! I'm really looking forward to it.

Engine 28: Something New You Learned

Jag lärde mig något nytt idag.	I learned something new today.
Jaså, vad då?	Oh, what did you learn?
Jag lärde mig att kaffets arom förändras mycket på bara fem minuter.	I learned that coffee's aroma changes a lot in just five minutes.
Oj, berätta mer!	Oh wow, tell me more!
Det beror på temperatur och syre i luften.	It depends on the temperature and air exposure.
Kommer det vara användbart i vardagen?	Will this be useful in daily life?
Kanske! Jag kanske börjar lukta på kaffe mer noggrant.	Maybe! Maybe I'll start smelling coffee more carefully.
Tack för att du delade, intressant!	Thanks for sharing, interesting!

Engine 29: Something You're Curious About

Jag är nyfiken på en sak.	I'm curious about one thing.
Jaså, vad funderar du på?	Oh, what are you wondering about?

Varför luktar vissa kaffesorter bättre än andra?	Why do some coffees smell better than others?
Intressant, vad fick dig att tänka på det?	Interesting, what made you think of that?
Jag märkte det i köket i morse.	I noticed it this morning in the kitchen.
Vad tror du själv?	What do you think?
Kanske rostningen eller färskheten?	Maybe the roast or freshness?
Om du tar reda på det, berätta för mig!	If you figure it out, tell me!
Självklart, nu fastnade det i tankarna.	Sure, now it stuck in my mind.

Engine 30: A Small Comfort or Treat You Enjoy

Jag har en liten vardagsgrej som jag verkligen gillar.	I have a small comfort I enjoy.
Åh, vad mysigt, vad är det?	Oh, lovely, what is it?
En varm kopp te på kvällen och en lugn stund utan telefon.	A warm tea in the evening and a quiet moment without my phone.
Är det ditt sätt att koppla av?	Is this your way to relax?
Ja, det lugnar sinnet.	Yes, it calms my mind.
Vad fint, små saker betyder mycket.	That’s lovely, small joys matter a lot.
Verkligen, det är dagens bästa stund.	Yes, it’s the best moment of the day.

Engine 31: Sharing Something You Noticed

Jag lade märke till en liten sak idag.	I noticed a small thing today.
Jaså, vad lade du märke till?	Oh, what did you notice?

Morgonhimlen var mycket ljusare än vanligt vid den här tiden.	The morning sky was much lighter than usual at that hour.
Varför fångade det din uppmärksamhet?	Why did it catch your attention?
Det såg ut som att våren var på väg.	It looked like spring was on the way.
Fin observation, vardagen är full av små detaljer.	Nice observation, everyday life is full of small details.
Ja, det gjorde hela dagen lite bättre.	It's, it brightened my whole day.

Engine 32: A Small Decision You Made Today

Jag tog ett litet beslut idag.	I made a small decision today.
Jaså, vad bestämde du dig för?	Oh, what did you decide?
Jag bestämde mig för att gå till jobbet i stället för att ta bussen.	I decided to walk to work instead of taking the bus.
Oj, varför då?	Oh, why so?
Jag ville ha lite frisk luft och rörelse.	I wanted some fresh air and movement.
Vad fick dig att ta det beslutet?	What made you decide this?
Jag kände mig trött på morgonen och tänkte att en promenad skulle hjälpa.	I felt tired in the morning and thought walking might help.
Det låter som en bra liten förändring.	Sounds like a good little change.
Ja, det gjorde dagen märkbart bättre.	Yes, it made the day noticeably better.

Engine 33: A Question You've Been Meaning to Ask

Jag har en liten fråga som jag har tänkt på.	I have a small question I've been thinking about.
Självklart, vad vill du fråga?	Of course, what do you want to ask?
Vilket café gillar du mest här i området?	Which café do you like most around here?
Varför undrar du det?	Why were you wondering?
Jag vill prova något nytt den här veckan.	I want to try something new this week.
Det var en bra fråga.	That was a good question.
Tack, jag fick en bra rekommendation.	Thanks, I got a good recommendation.

Engine 34: Sharing a Tiny Achievement

Jag fick en liten sak gjord idag.	I got one small thing done today.
Jaså, vad gjorde du?	Oh, what did you do?
Jag sorterade äntligen den där pappershögen på skrivbordet.	I finally sorted that stack of papers on my desk.
Hur kändes det?	How did it feel?
Förvånansvärt bra, som om en liten tyngd försvann.	Surprisingly good, like a small weight lifted.
Är det en del av ett större mål?	Is this part of a bigger goal?
Kanske, jag vill hålla arbetsplatsen i ordning.	Maybe, I want to keep my workspace tidy.
Vad bra, även små framsteg betyder mycket.	Great, even small successes matter a lot.
Tack! Det gjorde dagen bättre.	Thanks! It brightened my day.

Engine 35: Something You've Been Avoiding

Det finns en sak jag har skjutit upp ett tag.	There's something I've been putting off for a while.
Jaså, vad gäller det?	Oh, what is it?
Jag borde organisera en låda hemma.	I should organize one box at home.
Varför har det inte blivit gjort?	Oh, why hasn't it been done?
Det känns som en liten sak men ändå ganska jobbigt.	It feels small but tiring.
Skulle du kunna börja i liten skala?	Could you start it in a small step?
Kanske en hög i taget.	Maybe one pile at a time.
Bra att du tänker på det, även små steg räcker.	Good that you're thinking about it, even small progress is enough.
Sant, jag ska försöka ta tag i det imorgon.	True, I'll try to start it tomorrow.

Engine 36: A Small Joy or Surprise in Your Day

En liten, glad överraskning hände idag.	A small, happy surprise happened today.
Jaså, vad hände?	Oh, what happened?
Jag fick en liten gratis provflaska med juice på ett café.	I got a small sample bottle of a new juice at a café.
Vad härligt, vad var bäst med det?	Lovely, what was the best part?
Att det kom helt oväntat.	The fact that it was completely unexpected.

Hur kändes det mitt på dagen?	How did it feel in the middle of the day?
Det gjorde mig genast gladare.	It brightened me immediately.
Vad fint, små glädjeämnen gör dagen bättre.	Lovely, small joys make the day better.
Verkligen, små överraskningar är bäst.	They really do, little surprises are the best.

Engine 37: Something You're Thinking About Changing

Jag har funderat på en liten förändring i vardagen.	I've been thinking about making a small change in my routine.
Jaså, vad tänker du på?	Oh, what were you thinking about?
Jag funderar på att gå upp tio minuter tidigare.	I thought about waking up ten minutes earlier.
Varför vill du ändra det?	Why do you want to change that?
Det skulle kunna göra morgonen enklare.	It might make the morning easier.
Kan du börja med ett litet steg?	Could you start with a small step?
Ja, kanske bara fem minuter till att börja med.	Yes, maybe just a five-minute change at first.
Det låter som en bra idé, värt att prova.	Sounds like a good idea, worth trying.
Jag försöker nästa vecka!	I'll try next week!

Engine 38: Planning Something in the Near Future

Jag har en liten plan för den här veckan.	I have a small plan for this week.

Jaså, vad tänker du göra?	Oh, what are you planning to do?
Jag ska gå till biblioteket och lämna tillbaka ett par böcker.	I'm going to the library to return a couple of books.
Det låter bra, hur tänker du göra det?	Sounds nice, how will you do it?
Jag går dit efter jobbet.	I'll go after work.
Vad fick dig att planera det?	What made you plan this?
Jag vill börja veckan lugnt och strukturerat.	I want to start the week lightly and organized.
Jag hoppas att det går bra med planen.	I hope the plan goes well.
Tack, jag tror det också.	Thanks, I think it will.

Engine 39: Something You Appreciated Today

Jag uppskattade en liten sak idag.	I appreciated one small thing today.
Jaså, vad var det?	Oh, what was it?
Någon höll upp dörren för mig och log.	Someone opened a door for me and smiled.
Varför kändes det viktigt?	Why did it feel important?
Det var en så liten men vänlig gest.	It was such a small, kind gesture.
Var det en överraskning för dig?	Was this a surprise for you?
Lite, det gjorde mig genast gladare.	A little, it brightened my mood right away.
Vackert, små stunder av omtanke betyder mycket.	Beautiful, small moments of appreciation matter.
Verkligen, de påminner om att människor kan vara goda.	They really do, they remind me people can be good.

Engine 40: Something You're Curious to Try

Jag är nyfiken på att prova något snart.	I'm curious to try something soon.
Jaså, vad vill du prova?	Oh, what do you want to try?
Jag vill testa en ny promenadrutt nära mitt hem.	I want to try a new walking route near my home.
Varför just det?	Why this?
Det såg fint ut på kartan, en liten skogsstig.	It looked beautiful on the map, a small forest path.
Vad hoppas du få ut av det?	What do you hope to get from it?
Frisk luft och en ny utsikt.	Fresh air and a new view.
Det låter riktigt bra, absolut värt att prova!	Sounds really good, definitely worth trying!
Ja, kanske redan imorgon.	Yes, maybe I'll go tomorrow.

Engine 41: A Memory That Came to Mind

Idag kom ett minne upp i mitt sinne.	A memory came to my mind today.
Jaså, vilket minne?	Oh, what memory?
När jag var barn brukade vi dricka varm choklad under regniga kvällar.	As a child we used to drink hot cocoa on rainy evenings.
Vad fick dig att tänka på det?	What made you remember it?
Ljudet av regnet i morse gav samma känsla.	The sound of rain this morning brought back the vibe.
Är det ett viktigt minne för dig?	Is this an important memory for you?

Ja, det var alltid en lugn och varm stund.	Yes, it was always a peaceful, warm moment.
Vackert minne, tack för att du delade det.	A beautiful memory, thanks for sharing.
Varsågod, det kändes bra att minnas det.	You're welcome, it felt good to remember it.

Engine 42: Something Positive Noticed About Someone Else

Jag lade märke till något positivt hos dig idag.	I noticed something positive about you today.
Jaså, vad var det?	Oh, what was it?
Du har varit särskilt lugn och uppmuntrande idag.	You've been especially calm and encouraging today.
Vad fick dig att lägga märke till det?	What made you notice that?
Det märktes i hur du pratade med andra.	It showed in the way you spoke to others.
Är det typiskt för dig?	Is this typical for you?
Jag försöker hålla en lugn energi omkring mig.	I try to keep calm energy around me.
Jag ville bara säga det högt, bra energi sprider sig.	I just wanted to say it aloud, good energy spreads.
Tack, det betyder mycket.	Thank you, that means a lot.

Engine 43: Something You're Grateful For

Jag är tacksam för en liten sak idag.	I'm grateful for one small thing today.
Jaså, vad är du tacksam för?	Oh, what are you grateful for?
Jag är tacksam för att jag kunde dricka mitt morgonkaffe i lugn och ro.	I'm grateful that I had my morning coffee in peace.
Varför tänkte du på det just idag?	Why today?
Det gav morgonen en bra start.	It gave the morning a really good start.
Hur kändes dagen efter det?	How did the day feel afterward?
Lugnare och klarare.	Calmer and clearer.
Vackert, små stunder av tacksamhet stärker sinnet.	Beautiful, small gratitude moments strengthen the mind.
Ja, det var en bra påminnelse.	Yes, it was a good reminder.

Engine 44: Something That Caught Your Eye

Jag lade märke till något intressant omkring mig.	I noticed something interesting in my surroundings.
Jaså, vad lade du märke till?	Oh, what did you notice?
Ett vackert, gyllene ljus kom in genom fönstret.	A beautiful golden light came through the window.
Varför fångade det din uppmärksamhet?	What made it catch your attention?
Det var så mjukt och lugnande.	It was so soft and calming.
Förändrades stämningen när du såg det?	Did the atmosphere change when you noticed it?
Ja, stunden kändes lugnare.	Yes, the moment felt calmer.

Fin observation, små detaljer gör ögonblicket levande.	A beautiful observation, small details make the moment feel alive.
Det gör de verkligen, det var skönt att stanna upp en stund.	They truly do, it was good to pause for a moment.

Engine 45: A Small Preference You Have

Jag insåg att jag har en liten preferens.	I realized I have a small preference.
Jaså, vilken då?	Oh, what preference?
Jag tycker om att arbeta nära ett fönster.	I like working near a window.
Varför gillar du det?	Why do you like it?
Ljuset och utsikten gör att jag känner mig lättare.	The light and the view make me feel lighter.
Hur får det dig att känna?	How does it make you feel?
Mer fokuserad och avslappnad.	More focused and more relaxed.
Trevligt att höra, små preferenser gör vardagen personlig.	Nice to hear, small preferences make everyday life feel personal.
Ja, det är en liten men viktig sak för mig.	They really do, it's a small but important thing for me.

Engine 46: Something You're Looking Forward To

Jag ser fram emot en liten sak snart.	I'm looking forward to one small thing soon.
Jaså, vad ser du fram emot?	Oh, what are you looking forward to?
Jag ser fram emot en lugn kvällspromenad imorgon.	I'm looking forward to a calm evening walk tomorrow.

Varför känns det viktigt?	Why does this feel important?
Det hjälper mig att slappna av och rensa tankarna.	It relaxes me and clears my thoughts.
Hur tror du att det kommer att kännas?	How do you think it will feel?
Lugnt och uppfriskande.	Peaceful and refreshing.
Härligt, det är viktigt att ha något att se fram emot.	Wonderful, it's important to have things to look forward to.
Ja, bara tanken känns bra.	Yes, even thinking about it feels good.

Engine 47: Something That Recently Inspired You

Något litet inspirerade mig nyligen.	Something small recently inspired me.
Jaså, vad inspirerade dig?	Oh, what inspired you?
Jag hörde en tanke om hur små rutiner kan förändra dagen.	I heard a short idea about how small routines can change your day.
Varför just det?	Why that?
Det kändes enkelt och genomförbart.	It felt simple and doable.
Gav det dig en ny idé eller riktning?	Did it give you a new idea or direction?
Ja, jag vill prova en liten förändring i mina morgnar.	Yes, I want to try a small change in my mornings.
Härligt, inspiration kan räcka långt.	Wonderful, moments of inspiration carry far.
Ja, den här lilla idén fastnade verkligen.	True, the small idea really stuck with me.

Engine 48: A Question You've Been Thinking About

Jag har tänkt på en fråga den senaste tiden.	I've been thinking about one question lately.
Jaså, vilken fråga?	Oh, what question?
Jag undrar varför vissa dagar känns lätta utan tydlig anledning.	I've been wondering why some days feel light for no clear reason.
Hur kom du att tänka på det?	How did this come to mind?
Jag märkte igår att en liten sak gjorde hela dagen lättare.	I noticed yesterday that a small thing made the entire day easier.
Varför känns frågan viktig?	Why does this question feel important?
Kanske för att jag vill förstå vad som skapar välmående.	Maybe because I want to understand what creates well-being.
Bra fråga, den är värd att utforska i lugn och ro.	Great question, worth exploring at your own pace.
Ja, kanske hittar jag svaret med tiden.	True, maybe I'll find the answer over time.

Engine 49: Something You Recently Learned

Jag lärde mig något intressant nyligen.	I recently learned something interesting.
Jaså, vad lärde du dig?	Oh, what did you learn?
Jag lärde mig att en kort promenad kan förbättra koncentrationen i upp till en timme.	I learned that a short walk can improve focus for up to an hour.
Hur fick du veta det?	How did this come up? (How did you find out about it?)
Jag läste en kort artikel om det i morse.	I read a short article about it this morning.
Varför fastnade det hos dig?	Why did it stick?

För att det kändes enkelt och användbart.	Because it felt simple and useful.
Trevligt att höra om nytt lärande, det smittar.	It's nice to hear about new learning, it's contagious.
Ja, jag ska prova det imorgon.	Yes, I'm going to try it tomorrow.

Engine 50: A Small Improvement You Made Recently

Jag gjorde nyligen en liten förbättring i min vardag.	I recently made a small improvement in my daily life.
Jaså, vad förbättrade du?	Oh, what did you improve?
Jag organiserade mitt skrivbord så att allt viktigt är inom räckhåll.	I organized my desk so the important things are within reach.
Vad fick dig att göra det?	What made you do that?
Jag ville ha mer tydlighet och färre distraktioner.	I wanted more clarity and fewer distractions.
Märkte du någon skillnad?	Did you notice a difference?
Ja, arbetet känns lugnare nu.	Yes, working feels calmer now.
Bra gjort, små förbättringar gör stor skillnad.	Great, small improvements make a big difference.
Sant, det här var en bra början.	True, this was a good start.

Engine 51: Something You Fixed or Solved Recently

Jag löste nyligen ett litet problem.	I recently solved a small problem.
Jaså, vad fixade du?	Oh, what did you fix?
Jag fick äntligen datorns ljud att fungera ordentligt.	I finally got the computer sound working properly.

Vad var det som var fel?	What was wrong with it?
En inställning hade ändrats efter en uppdatering.	A setting had switched after an update.
Var det lätt eller svårt att fixa?	Was it easy or difficult?
Jag behövde bara hitta rätt inställning, det tog en stund.	I just needed to find the right option, it took a moment.
Hur kändes det att få det löst?	How did it feel?
Förvånansvärt bra, ett litet problem, stor lättnad.	Surprisingly good, small problem, big relief.
Bra gjort, små lösningar ger stor lättnad.	Great, small fixes bring big relief.
Ja, vardagen fungerar bättre nu.	Yes, daily life works better now.

Engine 52: A Small Habit You're Working On

Jag jobbar just nu på en liten vana.	I'm working on a small habit right now.
Jaså, vilken vana försöker du utveckla?	Oh, what habit are you working on?
Jag försöker dricka ett glas vatten direkt när jag vaknar.	I'm trying to drink a glass of water first thing in the morning.
Varför just den vanan?	Why this habit?
Jag ville börja dagen med en klarare känsla.	I wanted to start the day feeling a bit clearer.
Har det hjälpt?	Has it helped?
Ja, jag känner mig lättare och mer alert.	Yes, I feel lighter and more alert.
Bra mål, små vanor skapar stora förändringar.	Great goal, small habits create big changes.
Det gör de, det här känns som en bra början.	They do, this feels like a good start.

Engine 53: A Routine You Enjoy

Jag har en vardagsrutin som jag verkligen tycker om.	I have a daily routine I especially enjoy.
Jaså, vilken rutin?	Oh, what routine?
Jag dricker en kopp te varje kväll innan jag går och lägger mig.	I drink a cup of tea every evening before bed.
Varför gillar du den?	Why do you like it?
Den lugnar mig och markerar slutet på dagen.	It calms me and marks the end of the day.
Har det varit en del av ditt liv länge?	Has this been part of your life for long?
Ja, i flera år nu.	Yes, for several years now.
Vad fint, sådana rutiner gör vardagen mer balanserad.	Lovely, routines like this make daily life balanced.
Precis, det gör kvällarna lugnare.	Exactly, it gives the evening a peaceful moment.

Engine 54: Noticing Something Interesting About People

Jag märkte nyligen något intressant om människor.	I recently noticed something interesting about people.
Jaså, vad märkte du?	Oh, what did you notice?
Jag märkte att människor ofta ler när de hör någon skratta.	I noticed that people often smile when they hear someone else laugh.
Hur kom det sig?	How did this come up?

Jag hörde någon skratta på gatan, och flera förbipasserande log.	I heard someone laughing on the street, and several passersby smiled.
Har du sett det ofta?	Have you seen this often?
Ja, det verkar smitta av sig.	Yes, it seems contagious.
Fin iakttagelse, det finns alltid något nytt att lägga märke till hos människor.	Nice observation, there's always something new to notice about people.
Sant, små ögonblick säger mycket.	True, small moments reveal a lot.

Engine 55: Something That Made You Smile Recently

Jag log åt en liten sak idag.	I smiled today at one small thing.
Jaså, vad fick dig att le?	Oh, what made you smile?
Jag såg en liten hund springa vilt i snön.	I saw a small dog running wildly in the snow.
Hur kändes det?	What did the moment feel like?
Det var så spontant och glädjefyllt.	It was so spontaneous and joyful.
Varför kändes det så bra?	Why did that feel good?
Det väckte en känsla av barnslig glädje.	It brought out a sense of childlike joy.
Härligt, små stunder av glädje räcker långt.	Lovely, small smile moments carry far.
Det gör de, det gjorde hela dagen bättre.	They do, it brightened the whole day.

Engine 56: A Nice View or Visual Moment You Noticed

Jag såg ett vackert ögonblick idag.	I saw a beautiful moment today.
Jaså, hur såg det ut?	Oh, what was the view like?
Solen stod lågt och gav träden ett gyllene sken.	The sun was low and cast a golden glow on the trees.
Vad fick dig att lägga märke till det?	What made it catch your attention?
Ljuset var så mjukt och varmt.	The light was so soft and warm.
Hur var stämningen i stunden?	What was the atmosphere like?
Lugn, som om tiden saktade ner.	Peaceful, like time had slowed down.
Vacker iakttagelse, sådana stunder gör vardagen lugnare.	A beautiful observation, moments like these make daily life calmer.
Det gör de, det stannade kvar hos mig hela dagen.	They do, it stayed with me all day.

Engine 57: Something That Surprised You In a Good Way

Jag blev nyligen positivt överraskad av något.	I was recently surprised by something good.
Jaså, vad hände?	Oh, what happened?
En vän kom med kaffe till mig utan att jag bad om det.	A friend brought me a coffee without me asking.
Varför var det en överraskning?	Why was it a surprise?
Jag förväntade mig det inte alls, det var helt spontant.	I didn't expect it at all, it was completely spontaneous.
Hur kändes det?	How did it feel?
Varmt, som en liten gest av omtanke.	Heartwarming, like a small sign of care.
Härligt, sådana överraskningar gör dagen speciell.	Wonderful, good surprises make a day special.

Det gör de, det gjorde hela morgonen bättre.	They do, it brightened the whole morning.

Engine 58: Something You Changed Your Mind About

Jag ändrade nyligen uppfattning om något.	I recently changed my mind about something.
Jaså, om vad då?	Oh, what did you change your mind about?
Jag brukade tycka att tidiga morgnar var hemska, men nu märker jag att jag faktiskt gillar dem.	I used to think waking up early was terrible, but now I notice I actually like early mornings.
Vad fick dig att ändra synsätt?	What shifted your perspective?
Jag insåg att en lugn morgon ger en bättre start på dagen.	I realized that a calm morning gives a better start to the day.
Hur kändes den förändringen?	How did this change feel?
Förvånansvärt befriande, som att hitta en ny rytm.	Surprisingly freeing, like discovering a new rhythm.
Fin insikt, att ändra uppfattning kräver flexibilitet.	Great insight, changing your mind takes flexibility.
Det stämmer, förändringen kändes bra.	True, the shift felt good.

Engine 59: Something You Realized About Yourself

Jag insåg nyligen något om mig själv.	I recently realized something about myself.
Jaså, vad märkte du?	Oh, what did you notice?
Jag märkte att ett lugnt tempo passar mig bättre än stress.	I noticed that a calm pace suits me better than rushing.

Vad fick dig att inse det?	What made you realize it?
En dag var ovanligt stressig, och det kändes som fel rytm.	One day was unusually busy, and it just felt like the wrong rhythm.
Är det något nytt för dig?	Is this new for you?
Delvis, men nu förstår jag det tydligare.	Partly, but now I understand it more clearly.
Bra insikt, att känna sig själv är värdefullt.	Good insight, knowing yourself is valuable.
Det är det, det kändes viktigt att inse.	It's, it felt important to notice it.

Engine 60: Something You're Hoping For

Jag hoppas på en liten sak idag.	I'm hoping for one small thing today.
Jaså, vad hoppas du på?	Oh, what are you hoping for?
Jag hoppas att jag hinner ta en promenad innan kvällen.	I hope I have time for a walk before evening.
Varför just det?	Why that?
En promenad hjälper mig att rensa tankarna.	Walking helps clear my mind.
Hur skulle det kännas om det blir av?	How would it feel if it happens?
Lugn och uppfriskande.	Peaceful and refreshing.
Jag hoppas att det blir av, det låter viktigt.	I hope your wish comes true, it sounds important.
Tack, det vore ett fint avslut på dagen.	Thank you, it would be a nice end to the day.

Engine 61: Something That Motivates You Lately

En liten sak har motiverat mig på sistone.	One small thing has been motivating me lately.
Jaha, vad motiverar dig?	Oh, what motivates you?
Att jag märker små framsteg varje dag.	Noticing small progress every day.
Var kom den här motivationen ifrån?	Where did it come from?
Jag insåg att små framgångar ökar min energi.	I realized that small successes increase my energy.
Hur visar det sig i din vardag?	How does this show up in your daily life?
Jag börjar med uppgifter snabbare och tänker inte för mycket.	I start tasks more quickly and overthink less.
Fint att höra, motivation gör vardagen lättare.	Great, motivation makes daily life lighter.
Ja, det här känns som en bra riktning.	Yes, this feels like a good direction.

Engine 62: Something You Handled Better Than Expected

Jag hanterade nyligen en sak bättre än jag förväntade mig.	I handled something recently better than I expected.
Jaha, vad var det?	Oh, what was it?
Jag hanterade ett svårt telefonsamtal förvånansvärt smidigt.	I handled a difficult phone call surprisingly smoothly.
Varför trodde du först att det skulle bli svårt?	Why did you expect it to be hard?
För att jag tidigare brukade känna mig nervös i sådana situationer.	Because I used to feel nervous in situations like that.
Vad hjälpte dig att lyckas?	What helped you succeed?
Jag andades lugnt och talade tydligt.	I took a breath and spoke clearly.

Bra gjort, sådana stunder bygger självförtroende.	Great, moments like this build confidence.
Sant, det kändes som ett verkligt framsteg.	True, it felt like real progress.

Engine 63: Something You Want to Get Better At

Jag skulle vilja bli bättre på en sak.	I'd like to get better at something.
Jaha, vad skulle du vilja bli bättre på?	Oh, what would you like to get better at?
Jag skulle vilja lära mig att börja med uppgifter snabbare.	I'd like to learn to start tasks more quickly.
Varför just det?	Why that?
Jag märkte att jag skjuter upp små saker i onödan.	I noticed I postpone small things unnecessarily.
Vad skulle hjälpa dig att bli bättre?	What would help you improve?
Kanske korta rutiner eller en tydlig startpunkt.	Maybe short routines or a clear start time.
Det är ett bra mål, även små framsteg för dig framåt.	Great goal, even small progress moves you forward.
Tack, jag tänker likadant.	Thanks, I feel the same.

Engine 64: Something You Don't Enjoy, But May Need to Do

Det finns en sak som jag inte särskilt tycker om, men som ändå måste göras.	There's one thing I don't enjoy, but still need to do.
Jaha, vad är det?	Oh, what is it?
Pappersarbete, det tar min energi.	Paperwork, it drains my energy.

Varför tycker du inte om det?	Why don't you like it?
Det känns långsamt och splittrat.	It feels slow and scattered.
Vad är mest irriterande med det?	What's the most annoying part?
Att börja, tröskeln är alltid högst.	Getting started, the threshold is always the hardest.
Jag förstår helt, alla har sådana saker.	Totally get it, everyone has tasks like that.
Precis, men när det är gjort känns det lättare.	True, but once it's done, I feel lighter.

Engine 65: Something That Frustrated You Briefly But You Got Over It

Jag upplevde en liten frustration idag, men den gick snabbt över.	I had a small moment of frustration today, but it passed quickly.
Jaha, vad irriterade dig?	Oh, what annoyed you?
Min telefon låste inte upp direkt även om jag försökte flera gånger.	My phone wouldn't unlock right away even though I tried several times.
Var det oväntat?	Was it unexpected?
Ja, den brukar fungera direkt.	Yes, it usually works instantly.
Vad hjälpte dig att komma över det?	What helped you get over it?
Jag tog ett djupt andetag och skrattade åt situationen.	I took a deep breath and laughed at it.
Bra att du gick vidare så snabbt.	Good that you moved on quickly.
Ja, det var till slut bara en liten sak.	Yes, it was just a tiny thing in the end.

Engine 66: Something That Made You Smile Today

Idag fick en liten sak mig att le.	One small thing made me smile today.
Jaha, vad fick dig att le?	Oh, what made you smile?
En liten hund hoppade glatt i snön.	A little dog was happily bouncing in the snow.
Var det oväntat?	Was it unexpected?
Ja, det var så spontant och roligt.	Yes, it was so spontaneous and funny.
Varför fastnade just det här ögonblicket hos dig?	Why did this moment stick with you?
Det fanns något rent och lätt i det.	There was something pure and light about it.
Underbart, sådana stunder gör dagen lättare.	Lovely, moments like this make the day lighter.
Det gör de, det lyfte mitt humör direkt.	They do, it lifted my mood immediately.

Engine 67: Something You Appreciated Today

Jag uppskattade en liten sak idag.	I appreciated one small thing today.
Jaha, vad uppskattade du?	Oh, what did you appreciate?
Jag uppskattade att någon öppnade dörren för mig med ett leende.	I appreciated someone opening the door for me with a smile.
Var det en liten eller stor sak?	Was it small or big?
Liten, men den värmde ändå.	Small, but it warmed me anyway.
Var någon annan inblandad?	Did it involve someone else?
Ja, en helt främmande person, men vänlig.	Yes, a complete stranger, but kind.

Vackert, uppskattning gör vardagen mer meningsfull.	Beautiful, appreciation makes everyday life more meaningful.
Det gör det, det lyfte mitt humör direkt.	It does, it lifted my mood instantly.

Engine 68: Something You Noticed Today - Observation, Not Opinion

---

Jag lade märke till en liten sak omkring mig idag.	I noticed one small thing around me today.
Jaha, vad lade du märke till?	Oh, what did you notice?
Solen kom fram en stund mellan molnen och lyste upp hela gatan.	The sun came through the clouds for a moment and lit up the whole street.
Var var du då?	Where were you?
Ute på en promenad, det var ett väldigt ljust ögonblick.	On a walk, it was a very bright moment.
Hur såg det ut?	How did it look?
Ljuset var mjukt, nästan gyllene.	The light was soft, almost golden.
Vacker iakttagelse, små detaljer skapar lugn.	Beautiful observation, small details bring peace.
Det gör de, det fick mig att stanna upp en stund.	They do, it made me pause for a moment.

Engine 69: Something You Wondered About Today

Jag funderade på en liten sak idag.	I wondered about one small thing today.
Jaha, vad funderade du på?	Oh, what were you wondering about?

Jag undrade varför fåglar föredrar ett träd på gatan mer än de andra.	I wondered why birds prefer one tree on the street over the others.
Varför kom just det upp i tankarna?	Why did this come to mind?
Jag hörde nästan alla ljud från ett håll.	I heard almost all the sound coming from one direction.
Kom någon möjlig förklaring till dig?	Did any possible answer come to mind?
Jag tänkte att det kanske ger bättre skydd.	I guessed maybe that tree has better shelter.
Fin stund, lite förundran håller sinnet levande.	Nice moment, small wonder keeps the mind alive.
Sant, det gjorde promenaden mer intressant.	True, it made the walk more interesting.

Engine 70: Something You Found Interesting Recently

Jag hittade nyligen något intressant.	I found something interesting recently.
Jaha, vad hittade du?	Oh, what did you find?
Jag lärde mig att koltrastar ändrar sin sång lite när våren går framåt.	I learned that blackbirds slightly change their song as spring goes on.
Var stötte du på det?	Where did you come across that?
Jag hörde det i ett radioprogram.	I heard it on a radio program.
Vad var mest överraskande med det?	What surprised you most?
Jag visste inte att deras sånger förändras med årstiderna.	I didn't know their songs shift with the seasons.
Intressant, sådana upptäckter berikar vardagen.	Interesting, discoveries like that enrich daily life.

Det gör de, det fick mig att lyssna på fåglar på ett annat sätt.	They do, it made me listen to birds differently.

Engine 71: Something You Would Recommend to Someone

Jag har en liten rekommendation som kan vara till nytta.	I have a small recommendation that might be useful.
Jaha, vad skulle du rekommendera?	Oh, what would you recommend?
En kort stund av stretching direkt på morgonen, bara en minut.	A short stretching moment first thing in the morning, just one minute.
Varför just det?	Why that one?
Det väcker kroppen och klarnar sinnet utan ansträngning.	It wakes up the body and clears the mind with almost no effort.
När fungerar det bäst?	When does it work best?
Särskilt de dagar när man känner sig lite seg.	Especially on days when you feel a bit sluggish.
Det låter bra, små rekommendationer är ofta de bästa.	Sounds great, small recommendations are often the best.
Det är de, de är lätta att ta till sig.	They are, easy to adopt.

Engine 72: Something You've Been Enjoying Lately

Jag har på sistone njutit av en liten sak.	I've been enjoying one small thing lately.
Jaha, vad är det?	Oh, what is it?
Kvällspromenader direkt efter solnedgången.	Evening walks right after sunset.

Är det något nytt för dig?	Is that new for you?
Inte riktigt, men först nu har jag insett hur lugnande det är.	Not entirely, but only now have I realized how calming it is.
Vad tycker du mest om med det?	What appeals to you most?
Tystnaden och det mjuka ljuset.	The quiet and the soft light.
Underbart, sådant som ger glädje är viktigt.	Lovely, joy-giving things matter.
Det är det, det har blivit dagens bästa stund.	They do, it's become the best moment of my day.

Engine 73: Something You'd Like to Try Soon

Jag skulle vilja prova en liten sak snart.	I'd like to try one small thing soon.
Jaha, vad skulle du vilja prova?	Oh, what would you like to try?
Jag skulle vilja prova en ny frukostrutin, något lätt men varmt.	I'd like to try a new breakfast routine, something light but warm.
Varför just det?	Why that?
Jag vill ha en lugnare start på dagen.	I want a calmer start to the day.
Skulle du kunna börja redan idag eller imorgon?	Could you start today or tomorrow?
Förmodligen, jag behöver bara välja ett recept.	Probably, I just have to pick a recipe.
Det låter bra, nya försök ger energi.	Sounds good, new experiments bring energy.
Det gör de, en liten förändring piggar upp vardagen.	They do, even a small change brightens everyday life.

Engine 74: Something You Prefer (But Don't Always Get)

Jag har en liten preferens som jag inte alltid får.	I have a small preference I don't always get.
Jaha, vilken preferens är det?	Oh, what preference is that?
Jag gillar att sitta vid fönstret på kaféer.	I like sitting by the window in cafés.
Varför just det?	Why that?
Jag gillar ljuset och att kunna se ut.	I like the light and being able to see outside.
Hur känns det när du får det?	How does it feel when you get it?
Lugnande, som en liten stund för mig själv.	Calming, like a small moment of my own.
Jag förstår, små preferenser ger glädje i vardagen.	I understand, small preferences add joy to daily life.
Det gör de, det gör kaffestunden bättre.	They do, it makes the coffee moment better.

Engine 75: Something You Usually Choose Between Two Options

Jag väljer ofta ett visst alternativ mellan två.	I often choose one particular option between two.
Jaha, vilka alternativ?	Oh, which options?
Att ta trapporna eller hissen.	Taking the stairs, or the elevator.
Vilket väljer du oftast?	Which one do you usually choose?
Oftast trapporna.	Usually the stairs.
Varför just det?	Why that?

Det känns snabbare och lättare.	It feels quicker and lighter.
Roligt hur små vanor säger mycket om oss.	Funny how small habits say a lot about us.
Det gör de, det är bara mitt lilla val.	They do, it's just my little choice.

Engine 76: Something You Do Almost Every Day (But Isn't a "Habit" Yet)

Jag gör en liten sak nästan varje dag, även om jag inte skulle kalla det en vana ännu.	I do one small thing almost every day, though I wouldn't call it a habit yet.
Jaha, vad gör du nästan varje dag?	Oh, what do you do almost every day?
Jag dricker en kopp te på eftermiddagen.	I have a cup of tea in the afternoon.
När började du med det?	When did you start?
Kanske för ett par månader sedan.	Maybe a couple of months ago.
Varför tror du att det ännu inte har blivit en vana?	Why hasn't it become a habit yet?
Ibland är dagarna annorlunda och tiden räcker inte till.	Some days are different and time slips by.
Det låter som ett fint litet tillskott i vardagen.	Sounds like a nice little addition to your day.
Ja, det är en lugn stund när jag hinner.	Yes, it's a peaceful moment when I have time.

Engine 77: Something You Don't Do Often, But Enjoy Every Time

Det finns en sak jag inte gör ofta, men som jag alltid tycker om.	There's one thing I don't do often, but enjoy every time.
Jaha, vad gör du sällan men tycker om att göra?	Oh, what do you do rarely but enjoy doing?
Jag åker en lång bussresa utan brådska.	I take a long bus ride with no hurry.
När gjorde du det senast?	When did you last do it?
Förra månaden, det var en regnig dag och det kändes rätt.	Last month, it was a rainy day and it felt right.
Vad är det bästa med det?	What's the best part?
Den lugna rörelsen och landskapet som förändras.	The gentle movement and changing scenery.
Härligt att du har en sådan "liten lyx".	Lovely that you have this little "luxury."
Ja, det känns alltid speciellt.	Yes, it always feels special.

Engine 78: Something That Comforts You

Det finns en liten sak som tröstar mig.	There's one small thing that comforts me.
Jaha, vad är det som tröstar dig?	Oh, what is that comfort?
En varm dryck i handen, te eller kakao.	A warm drink in my hand, tea or cocoa.
När märkte du att det fungerar?	When did you realize this works?
För flera år sedan, det lugnar mig direkt.	Years ago, it soothes me instantly.
Hur känns den här trösten?	What does the comfort feel like?
Mjuk, trygg, som en liten vilostund.	Soft, safe, like a little moment of rest.

Underbart att du har en sådan liten tröst.	Lovely that you have this small comfort.
Ja, det hjälper mig att hitta balansen igen.	It does, it helps me find balance again.

Engine 79: Something You Love the Sound Of

Jag älskar att lyssna på ett visst ljud.	I love the sound of something.
Jaha, vilket ljud?	Oh, which sound?
Regnets smattrande mot fönstret.	Rain tapping against the window.
När märker du det mest?	When do you notice it most?
På kvällarna, när det är tyst.	In the evenings, when it's quiet.
Finns det något minne kopplat till det?	Is there a memory connected to it?
Kanske från barndomen, regniga dagar kändes alltid lugna.	Maybe from childhood, rainy days always felt calm.
Vackert val, ljud kan vara oväntat tröstande.	Beautiful choice, sounds can be surprisingly comforting.
Det kan de, det får mig att känna mig mjuk och lugn.	They can, it makes me feel soft and peaceful.

Engine 80: Something You Love the Look Of

Jag tycker särskilt mycket om hur något ser ut.	I really like the look of something.
Jaha, vad menar du?	Oh, what do you mean?
En solnedgång över vatten.	A sunset over water.
När ser det som bäst ut?	When does it look the best?

När färgerna skiftar långsamt från orange till lila.	When the colors shift slowly from orange to purple.
Finns det en historia kopplad till den synen?	Is there a story connected to this sight?
Som barn brukade jag titta ut över sjön på kvällarna, det kändes oändligt.	As a child I used to look at the lake in the evenings, it felt endless.
Vackert val, visuella stunder stannar kvar hos oss.	Beautiful choice, visual moments stay with us.
Det gör de, det ger alltid en liten känsla av lugn.	They do, it always brings a little peace.

Engine 81: Something You Love the Smell Of

Jag älskar doften av en sak.	I love the smell of something.
Jaha, vilken doft?	Oh, what smell?
Doften av nybryggt kaffe på morgonen.	The smell of fresh coffee in the morning.
När doftar det som bäst?	When does it smell the best?
Precis innan första klunken.	Right before the first sip.
Finns det något minne kopplat till det?	Is there a memory connected to it?
Kanske från studietiden, kaffe betydde början på dagen.	Maybe from my student years, coffee signaled the start of the day.
Fint val, dofter väcker minnen snabbt.	Lovely choice, scents awaken memories quickly.
Det gör de, och den här doften är alltid tröstande.	They do, and this one is always comforting.

Engine 82: Something You Like the Feel Of (Sensation)

Jag gillar känslan av en sak.	I like the feel of something.
Jaha, känslan av vad?	Oh, the feel of what?
En varm mugg en kall morgon.	A warm mug on a cold morning.
Hur känns det exakt?	What does it feel like exactly?
Det är en lugnande, mjuk värme i handen.	A calming, soft warmth in my hand.
Hjälper det dig att slappna av?	Does it help soothe you?
Ja, det får mig att känna mig mer avslappnad direkt.	Yes, it makes me feel more relaxed right away.
Fint val, texturer påverkar verkligen humöret.	Beautiful choice, textures really do affect mood.
Sant, en liten men betydelsefull känsla.	True, a small but meaningful feeling.

Engine 83: A Temperature or Weather Feeling You Really Enjoy

Jag tycker verkligen om en viss typ av väderkänsla.	I really like a certain kind of weather feeling.
Jaha, vilken typ av känsla?	Oh, what kind of feeling?
Jag tycker om den svala morgonluften, precis före soluppgången.	I enjoy the cool morning air right before sunrise.
När känns det som bäst?	When does it feel the best?
När världen fortfarande är tyst.	When the world is still quiet.
Varför tilltalar just den här känslan dig?	Why does this feeling appeal to you?

Den påminner mig om en ny början varje dag.	It reminds me of a fresh start each day.
Fint val, väderkänslor kan vara oväntat tröstande.	Beautiful choice, weather feelings can be comforting.
Ja, den får mig att känna mig klar och lugn.	Yes, it makes me feel clear and peaceful.

Engine 84: A Kind of Light You Love (Morning, Evening, Indoors, Night)

Jag älskar en viss sorts ljus.	I love a certain kind of light.
Jaha, vilken sorts ljus menar du?	Oh, what kind?
Det mjuka, gyllene ljuset vid solnedgången.	The soft, golden light of sunset.
Ser det bäst ut på kvällen?	Does it look best in the evening?
Ja, när alla färger känns varma.	Yes, when all the colors feel warm.
Finns det ett minne kopplat till det ljuset?	Is there a memory tied to it?
Sommarkvällar från barndomen vid sjön.	Childhood summer evenings by the lake.
Fint val, ljus påverkar alltid stämningen.	Beautiful choice, light always shapes the mood.
Det får mig att känna mig lugn varje gång.	It makes me feel peaceful every time.

Engine 85: A Time of Day You Really Enjoy

Det finns en tid på dagen som jag verkligen tycker om.	There's a time of day I especially enjoy.
Jaha, vilken stund är det?	Oh, which moment?
Tidig morgon, när allt fortfarande är tyst.	Early morning, when everything is still quiet.
Hur känns det för dig?	How does it feel to you?
Lugn, klar, som en ny början.	Peaceful, clear, like a new beginning.
Varför är just den här stunden viktig för dig?	Why is this moment important?
Den ger mig några minuter av eget utrymme.	It gives me a few minutes of my own space.
Fint val, små stunder säger mycket om oss.	Beautiful choice, small moments say a lot about us.
Sant, det är dagens mildaste stund.	True, it's the gentlest moment of the day.

Engine 86: A Day of the Week That Feels Good to You and Why

Det finns en veckodag som alltid känns bra för mig.	There's one day of the week that always feels good to me.
Jaha, vilken dag är det?	Oh, which day?
Jag gillar torsdag, den har en känsla av att helgen närmar sig.	I like Thursday, it has a hint of weekend promise.
Hur känns den dagen för dig?	How does it feel to you?
Lätt och hoppfull.	Light and hopeful.
Varför sticker just den dagen ut?	Why does it stand out?

Det känns som att veckan redan är halvvägs förbi, men det finns fortfarande energi kvar.	It feels like the week is halfway behind me, yet there's still energy left.
Fint val, varje veckodag har sin egen rytm.	Beautiful choice, each day has its rhythm.
Sant, torsdag har alltid känts som en dag med bra flyt.	True, Thursday has always felt like a "good momentum" day.

Engine 87: A Season or Month That Feels Special to You

Det finns en årstid som känns speciell för mig.	There's one season that feels special to me.
Jaha, vilken årstid?	Oh, which season?
Jag gillar hösten, färgerna och svalkan känns bra.	I like autumn, the colors and coolness feel good to me.
Hur känns det för dig?	What does it feel like?
Lugn och klar, som en liten början.	Calm and clear, like a small beginning.
Finns det ett minne kopplat till det?	Is there a memory connected to it?
Ja, skolstart på hösten och krispiga morgnar.	Yes, the start-of-school autumns and crisp mornings.
Fint val, årstider påverkar oss mer än vi märker.	Beautiful choice, seasons shape us more than we realize.
Sant, hösten får mig att känna mig balanserad.	True, autumn makes me feel balanced.

Engine 88: A Place (Big or Small) That Makes You Feel Calm

Jag har en plats där jag känner mig lugn.	I have one place where I feel calm.
Jaha, vilken plats?	Oh, what place?
En liten bänk i parken, under en stor björk.	A small bench in a park, under a big birch tree.
Hur är den platsen?	What is it like?
Tyst, med ljus som silas genom grenarna.	Quiet, with light filtering through the branches.
Finns det ett minne kopplat till platsen?	Is there a memory tied to it?
Jag brukade gå dit under studietiden, det hjälpte mig att andas ut.	I used to go there during my studies, it helped me breathe.
Härligt val, lugna platser är viktiga i vardagen.	Lovely choice, calm places matter.
Ja, den platsen återställer alltid min balans.	Yes, that place always restores my balance.

Engine 89: Something You Enjoy Doing With Other People

Jag tycker om att göra en sak tillsammans med andra.	I enjoy doing something with other people.
Jaha, vad är det?	Oh, what is it?
Jag tycker om att laga mat tillsammans.	I like cooking together.
Vem gör du det helst med?	Who do you like doing it with?
Vänner, det är avslappnat och roligt.	Friends, it's relaxed and fun.
Varför känns det bättre tillsammans?	Why does it feel better together?
För att idéer och smaker växer fram tillsammans.	Because ideas and flavors develop together.

Fint val, gemensamma stunder stärker relationer.	Lovely choice, shared moments strengthen relationships.
Det gör de, att laga mat tillsammans är alltid en varm stund.	They do, cooking together is always a warm moment.

Engine 90: A Type of Conversation You Find Easy

Det finns en typ av samtal som känns lätt för mig.	There's a type of conversation that feels easy for me.
Jaha, vilken typ av samtal?	Oh, what kind?
Lätta, vardagliga samtal om små saker.	Light, everyday chats about small things.
Varför känns just den typen naturlig för dig?	Why does that feel natural?
För att det inte finns någon press, de bara flyter.	Because there's no pressure, they just flow.
Handlar lättheten mer om ämnet eller rytmen?	Is the ease about the topics or the rhythm?
Kanske rytmen, ett lugnt fram-och-tillbaka.	Probably the rhythm, a calm back-and-forth.
Fin insikt, naturliga samtal gör kontakt enklare.	Lovely insight, natural conversations make connection easier.
Det gör de, det är min komfortzon.	They do, they're my comfort zone.

Engine 91: A Type of Conversation You Find Challenging

Det finns en typ av samtal som känns utmanande för mig.	There's a type of conversation that feels challenging for me.

Jaha, vilken typ av samtal känns utmanande?	Oh, what kind?
Snabba, snabbt skiftande samtal där man pratar om många saker samtidigt.	Fast, rapidly changing conversations with many topics at once.
Handlar det om rytmen eller innehållet?	Is it the rhythm or the content?
Kanske rytmen, jag hinner inte alltid med.	Probably the rhythm, I don't always keep up.
Hur känns det för dig?	How does that feel to you?
Lite överväldigande, som att jag hela tiden ligger ett steg efter.	A bit overwhelming, like I'm always one step behind.
Fin insikt, att känna sina utmaningar är visdom.	A lovely insight, knowing your challenges is wisdom.
Tack, jag lär mig hela tiden hur jag kan vara lugnare i sådana situationer.	Thanks, I'm learning how to stay calmer in those situations.

Engine 92: Something You Appreciate in a Friend

Jag uppskattar en särskild egenskap hos en vän.	I appreciate one particular quality in a friend.
Jaha, vilken egenskap är det?	Oh, which quality?
Ärlighet, ett varmt och rakt sätt att prata.	Honesty, a warm, straightforward way of speaking.
Varför är det viktigt för dig?	Why is that important to you?
För att det får mig att känna mig trygg och uppskattad.	Because it makes me feel safe and valued.
Har det att göra med tillit?	Does this relate to trust?
Ja, ärlighet skapar en lugn kontakt.	Yes, honesty builds a calm connection.

Fin tanke, värderingar i vänskap säger mycket om oss.	Beautiful thought, friendship values say a lot.
Det gör de, de visar vilken sorts sällskap vi söker.	They do, they show what kind of company we seek.

Engine 93: Something You Notice in People Quickly

Jag lägger snabbt märke till en sak hos människor.	I notice one thing in people very quickly.
Jaha, vad är det?	Oh, what is it?
Hur de lyssnar, uppmärksamt eller distraherat.	Whether they listen attentively or distractedly.
Varför fångar det din uppmärksamhet?	Why does that catch your attention?
För att det påverkar rytmen i samtalet.	Because it influences the rhythm of the conversation.
Ger det dig ofta en riktig känsla?	Does this often give you an accurate intuition?
Oftast ja, att lyssna avslöjar mycket.	Often yes, listening reveals a lot.
Fin insikt, det gör samspelet mer medvetet.	A wonderful insight, it makes interaction more mindful.
Det gör det, det hjälper mig att hitta en bra kontakt.	It does, it helps me find a good connection.

Engine 94: How You Usually Introduce Yourself

Jag har ett sätt som jag brukar presentera mig på för nya människor.	I have one way I usually introduce myself to new people.
Jaha, hur brukar du göra?	Oh, how do you usually do it?

Jag börjar med mitt namn och säger kort vad jag gör.	I start with my name and briefly say what I do.
Är din presentation kort eller längre?	Is your introduction short or longer?
Kort, jag vill hålla den tydlig.	Short, I like keeping it clear.
Varför fungerar det för dig?	Why does that work for you?
För att samtalet sedan kan gå åt vilket håll som helst.	Because after that, the conversation can go anywhere.
Bra, att ha sitt sätt att presentera sig ger trygghet.	Great, knowing your introduction style builds confidence.
Det gör det, det hjälper mig att börja ett bra samtal.	It does, it helps me start a good conversation.

Engine 95: A Cultural Habit You Find Interesting

Det finns en kulturell vana som jag tycker är väldigt intressant.	There's a cultural habit I find very interesting.
Jaha, vilken vana är det?	Oh, which one?
Att man bugar som hälsning i Japan.	The way people bow as a greeting in Japan.
Var såg du det första gången?	Where did you first see it?
När jag reste, det kändes både vackert och respektfullt.	While traveling, it felt both beautiful and respectful.
Vad tror du att den vanan säger om kulturen?	What do you think that habit says about the culture?
Kanske respekt, noggrannhet och känsla för situationer.	Perhaps respect, precision, and awareness of context.
Fin iakttagelse, kulturella vanor öppnar nya perspektiv.	Beautiful insight, cultural habits open new perspectives.

Det gör de, små vanor avslöjar ibland mest.	They do, small habits sometimes reveal the most.

Engine 96: How You Like to Plan Your Week

Jag har ett eget sätt att planera min vecka.	I have my own way of planning my week.
Jaha, hur brukar du planera din vecka?	Oh, how do you usually plan it?
Jag gör en kort lista på söndagskvällar.	I make a short list on Sunday evenings.
Föredrar du en strikt plan eller en flexibel ram?	Do you prefer a strict schedule or a flexible outline?
En flexibel, jag vill ha utrymme för förändringar.	Flexible, I like room for changes.
Vad ger det dig?	What benefit does it give you?
Det lugnar sinnet och ger veckan en tydlig start.	It calms my mind and gives the week a clear start.
Bra, ett eget sätt att planera gör vardagen lättare.	Wonderful, having your own planning style makes daily life easier.
Det gör det, små rutiner skapar balans.	It does, and small routines bring balance.

Engine 97: A Habit You Want to Build or Improve

Det finns en vana som jag skulle vilja utveckla.	There's one habit I'd like to develop.
Jaha, vilken vana är det?	Oh, what habit?

Jag skulle vilja röra mig lite mer i vardagen.	I'd like to move a little more during the day.
Varför är det viktigt för dig?	Why is that important to you?
För att det ger mer energi och klarare tankar.	Because it boosts my energy and clears my mind.
Vad skulle det ge dig om det blev en vana?	What benefit would it bring if it became consistent?
Jag skulle känna mig mer i balans.	I'd feel more balanced.
Bra, små steg räcker när riktningen är rätt.	Wonderful, small steps are enough when the direction is right.
Ja, jag börjar lugnt och bygger vidare därifrån.	Yes, I'll start small and build from there.

Engine 98: A Piece of Advice You Often Give Others

Det finns ett råd som jag ofta ger.	There's one piece of advice I give often.
Jaha, vilket råd är det?	Oh, what is it? (Well, what advice is that?)
Att det är viktigt att vara snäll mot sig själv, även under stressiga dagar.	That it's important to be kind to yourself, even on busy days.
När brukar du ge det rådet?	When do you give this advice?
När någon är för hård mot sig själv.	When someone is too hard on themselves.
Kommer det från egna erfarenheter?	Does it come from your own experience?
Ja, jag lärde mig det när jag slutade lyssna på mina egna behov.	Yes, I learned it when I forgot to listen to my own needs.

Fint råd, det kan verkligen göra någons dag lättare.	Beautiful advice, it can truly lighten someone's day.
Jag hoppas det, vänlighet underskattas ofta.	I hope so, kindness is often underestimated.

Engine 99: A Small Dream You Hope to Fulfill Someday

Jag har en liten dröm som jag skulle vilja uppfylla en dag.	I have a small dream I'd like to fulfill someday.
Jaha, vad är det?	Oh, what is it?
Jag skulle vilja skriva en egen liten novellsamling.	I'd like to write my own small collection of stories.
Är det ett projekt eller mer en personlig önskan?	Is it a project or more of a personal wish?
Kanske båda, det är en viktig tanke för mig.	Maybe both, it's a meaningful idea for me.
Varför är just den drömmen viktig?	Why this dream?
För att berättelser alltid har följt mig.	Because stories have always been with me.
Fin dröm, varje steg tar dig närmare.	A beautiful dream, every step brings you closer.
Jag hoppas det, kanske vågar jag börja en dag.	I hope so, maybe one day I'll be brave enough to begin.

Engine 100: Something That Helps You Feel Grounded

Det finns något som hjälper mig att känna mig jordad.	There's something that helps me feel grounded.

Jaha, vad är det?	Oh, what is it?
En kort promenad utomhus, särskilt på morgonen.	A short walk outside, especially in the morning.
Känns det mer fysiskt eller mentalt jordande?	Does it feel physically or mentally grounding?
Båda, stegens rytm lugnar mig.	Both, the rhythm of the steps calms me.
Varför fungerar det så bra för dig?	Why does it work so well for you?
För att frisk luft och rörelse ger klarhet direkt.	Because fresh air and movement bring instant clarity.
Det är ett fint sätt att ta hand om sig själv.	A beautiful way to care for yourself.
Det är det, det håller mig i balans under stressiga dagar.	It is, it keeps me balanced on busy days.

Engine 101: How You Recharge After a Busy Day

Jag har ett sätt som hjälper mig att återhämta mig efter en hektisk dag.	I have a habit that helps me recharge after a busy day.
Jaha, vad hjälper dig att återhämta dig?	Oh, what helps you recharge?
En kort stund i tystnad, utan telefon eller ljud.	A short moment of quiet—no phone, no noise.
Gör du det varje dag eller ibland?	Do you do it daily or only sometimes?
Nästan varje dag, det är en del av min kvällsrutin.	Almost daily, it's part of my evening routine.
Hur känns den här vanan för dig?	How does this habit feel to you?

Den klargör tankarna och sänker pulsen.	It clears my thoughts and slows my heartbeat.
En fin vana, återhämtning är viktigt.	A great habit, recovery is important.
Ja, annars stannar dagen kvar som "påslagen".	It is, otherwise the day stays "switched on."

Engine 102: A Quality You Are Working to Strengthen in Yourself

Jag arbetar med att stärka en egenskap hos mig själv.	I'm working on strengthening one of my qualities.
Jaha, vilken egenskap är det?	Oh, which one?
Tålamod, jag vill förhålla mig lugnare till saker.	Patience, I want to approach things more calmly.
Varför är den egenskapen viktig för dig?	Why is this trait important to you?
För att jag ibland reagerar för snabbt under press.	Because under pressure I sometimes react too quickly.
Vad skulle det ge dig om du stärkte den?	What benefit would it bring?
Det skulle göra vardagen jämnare och tydligare.	It would make my daily life smoother and clearer.
Fint att du arbetar med det.	Wonderful that you're working on this.
Tack, jag tar små steg varje dag.	Thank you, I'm taking small steps every day.

Engine 103: A Sign That You Feel Comfortable With Someone

Jag märker ett tecken på att jag känner mig bekväm med någon.	I notice a sign that I feel comfortable with someone.
Jaha, vilket tecken?	Oh, what sign?
Jag börjar skratta lättare och mer spontant.	I start laughing more easily and spontaneously.
Märker andra det?	Do others notice it?
Oftast ja, det smittar.	Usually yes, it's contagious.
Varför visar det bekvämlighet?	Why does that show comfort?
För att spontant skratt bara kommer i en trygg miljö.	Because spontaneous laughter only comes in a safe atmosphere.
Fin insikt, det visar äkta kontakt.	A beautiful insight, it shows real connection.
Jag tycker det, då vet jag att jag är i gott sällskap.	I think so too, that's when I know I'm in good company.

Engine 104: A Routine That Makes Your Mornings Better

Jag har en morgonrutin som gör min dag bättre.	I have a morning routine that makes my day better.
Jaha, vilken rutin?	Oh, what routine?
Jag dricker ett glas vatten och andas lugnt en stund innan allt annat.	I drink a glass of water and breathe calmly before anything else.
Är det en kort eller längre stund?	Is it short or longer?
Kort, men det känns långt på ett bra sätt.	Short, but it feels long in a good way.

Hur känns det för dig?	How does it feel?
Klargörande, som om en tyngd faller från axlarna.	Clarifying, like a weight drops off my shoulders.
Fin rutin, små handlingar gör morgnar tydligare.	Great routine, small actions make mornings clearer.
Ja, det ger hela dagen en bättre start.	Yes, it gives the whole day a better start.

Engine 105: A Value You Try to Live By

Jag försöker leva efter ett viktigt värde.	I try to live according to one important value.
Jaha, vilket värde?	Oh, which one?
Ärlighet, både mot mig själv och andra.	Honesty, toward myself and others.
Varifrån kommer det värdet?	Where did it come from?
Från barndomen, jag lärde mig det av mina föräldrar.	From childhood, I learned it from my parents.
Vad betyder det i vardagen?	What does it mean in daily life?
Att jag talar sanning och möter saker direkt men vänligt.	That I speak truthfully and face things directly but kindly.
Ett vackert värde, det speglar vem du är.	A beautiful value, it reflects who you are.
Jag hoppas det, det hjälper mig att hålla balansen.	I hope so, it helps me stay balanced.

Engine 106: Something You Admire in Other People

Det finns en egenskap hos människor som jag beundrar.	There's one quality in people that I admire.
Jaha, vilken egenskap?	Oh, which one?
Äkta vänlighet, ett lugnt och varmt sätt att möta andra.	Genuine kindness, a calm, warm way of meeting others.
Varför beundrar du det?	Why do you admire that?
För att vänlighet ibland känns sällsynt i världen.	Because kindness sometimes feels rare in the world.
Hur känns det att vara nära en sådan person?	How does it feel to be around someone like that?
Tryggt och uppskattat.	Safe and appreciated.
Fin insikt, det speglar dina egna värderingar.	Beautiful insight, it reflects your own values.
Jag tror det, därför berör det mig.	I think so, that's why it touches me.

Engine 107: Something You've Learned About Yourself

Jag har lärt mig något nytt om mig själv nyligen.	I've learned something new about myself recently.
Jaha, vad har du lärt dig?	Oh, what did you learn?
Att jag behöver fler tysta stunder än jag trodde.	That I need more quiet moments than I thought.
Överraskade det dig?	Did that surprise you?
Lite, jag märkte inte belastningen förrän jag stannade upp.	A little, I didn't notice the fatigue until I paused.
Varför tror du att det kom fram nu?	Why do you think it surfaced now?
För att livet hade varit för fullt för länge.	Because life had been too full for too long.

Fin insikt, självförståelse växer i små stunder.	A beautiful insight, self-understanding grows in small moments.
Ja, det här känns lugnande.	Yes, this realization feels calming.

Engine 108: Something New You Want to Learn This Year

Jag vill lära mig något nytt i år.	I want to learn something new this year.
Jaha, vad vill du lära dig?	Oh, what would you like to learn?
Jag vill lära mig att rita bättre skisser.	I'd like to learn to draw better sketches.
Är det en färdighet eller ett kreativt projekt?	Is it a skill or a creative project?
En kreativ färdighet, jag har alltid velat prova.	A creative skill, I've always wanted to try.
Vad skulle det ge dig?	What benefit would it bring?
Det skulle hjälpa mig att uttrycka idéer visuellt.	It would help me express ideas visually.
Ett fint mål, att lära sig något nytt ger året mening.	Wonderful goal, learning something new gives the year meaning.
Jag hoppas det, jag börjar med små övningar.	I hope so, I'll start with small exercises.

Engine 109: A Way You Like to Encourage Other People

Jag har ett sätt att uppmuntra andra.	I have one way I like to encourage others.
Jaha, vilket sätt?	Oh, what way?
Jag säger alltid en lugnande mening: "Du tar redan rätt steg."	I always say one calming phrase: "You're already taking the right steps."

Kommer det naturligt för dig?	Does it come naturally?
Ja, jag vill påminna människor om deras egen styrka.	Yes, I want to remind people of their own strength.
Varför känns det rätt för dig?	Why does that feel right to you?
För att det inte pressar, utan ger utrymme att andas.	Because it doesn't pressure, it gives room to breathe.
Ett fint sätt att uppmuntra, det visar empati.	A beautiful way to encourage, it reflects your empathy.
Jag hoppas att orden når fram i rätt ögonblick.	I hope the words reach people at the right moment.

Engine 110: A Sound That Makes You Feel Relaxed

Det finns ett ljud som får mig att känna mig avslappnad.	There's one sound that makes me relaxed.
Jaha, vilket ljud?	Oh, what sound?
Det stilla smattret av regn mot fönstret.	The soft patter of rain on a window.
Var hör du det oftast?	Where do you usually hear it?
Hemma, när allt annat är tyst.	At home, when everything else is quiet.
Hur känns det för dig?	How does it feel to you?
Som en mjuk andning som jämnar ut tankarna.	Like a gentle breath that smooths out my thoughts.
Ett vackert val, ljud kan vara mycket läkande.	A beautiful choice, sounds can be very healing.
Ja, det lugnar mig alltid.	Yes, it always calms me.

Engine 111: A Lesson You Learned the Hard Way

Jag har lärt mig en viktig sak den hårda vägen.	I've learned an important lesson the hard way.
Jaha, vad lärde du dig?	Oh, what did you learn?
Att man ibland måste kunna säga "nej", även när det känns svårt.	That sometimes you have to say "no," even when it feels difficult.
Vilken situation lärde dig detta?	What situation taught you this?
Jag överbelastade mig länge eftersom jag inte ville göra någon besviken.	I overloaded myself for a long time because I didn't want to disappoint anyone.
Varför tror du att det krävdes en svår situation?	Why did learning this require hardship?
För att jag först då insåg mina gränser när jag var riktigt utmattad.	Because I only recognized my limits when I was truly exhausted.
Svåra erfarenheter lär ofta de mest bestående sakerna.	Hard experiences often teach the most lasting lessons.
Ja, och nu kan jag ta bättre hand om mig själv.	Yes, and now I can take better care of myself.

Engine 112: A Small Joy From Your Week

Den här veckan hade jag en liten stund som gjorde mig glad.	This week I had a small moment that made me happy.
Jaha, vilken stund var det?	Oh, what moment was it?
Jag fick dricka mitt morgonkaffe i lugn och ro i solen.	I got to drink my morning coffee peacefully in the sun.
Hände det i vardagen eller i något speciellt sammanhang?	Did it happen during everyday life or something special?

I vardagen, och just därför kändes det så bra.	Everyday life, that's exactly why it felt so good.
Hur fick det dig att känna dig?	How did it make you feel?
Lugn och närvarande.	Calm and present.
En fin stund, små glädjeämnen gör livet lättare.	Lovely moment, small joys make life lighter.
Ja, vi borde lägga märke till dem oftare.	They do, we should notice them more often.

Engine 113: Something You Value in a Friendship

Det finns en sak i vänskap som jag verkligen värdesätter.	There's one thing I truly value in a friendship.
Jaha, vad är det?	Oh, what is it?
Ärlighet, att kunna prata öppet utan rädsla.	Honesty, being able to speak openly without fear.
Varför är det så viktigt för dig?	Why is that so important to you?
För att ärlighet bygger tillit, och utan den håller inte en vänskap.	Because honesty builds trust, and without it a friendship can't last.
Hur visar sig det i praktiken?	How does that show up in real life?
Att kunna säga sanningen vänligt och lyssna genuint.	In being able to tell the truth gently and listen genuinely.
Ett vackert värde, det säger mycket om hur du möter andra.	A beautiful value, it reflects how you meet others.
Jag tror det, det gör vänskap djupare.	I think so, it makes friendship deeper.

Engine 114: A Goal You Want to Focus on This Month

Den här månaden vill jag fokusera på ett viktigt mål.	This month I want to focus on one important goal.
Vilket mål är det?	What goal is it?
Jag vill förbättra min sömnrytm.	I want to improve my sleep schedule.
Varför är det viktigt just nu?	Why is it important now?
För att jag har varit trött länge och vill ha mer energi i vardagen.	Because I've been tired for a long time and want more energy for daily life.
Vilka steg kan du ta?	What steps could you take?
Gå och lägga mig vid samma tid och minska skärmtid på kvällen.	Go to bed at the same time and reduce screen time in the evening.
Ett bra mål, en månad räcker för att se förändring.	Great goal, a month is enough to see a real difference.
Jag hoppas det, små rutiner kan hjälpa mycket.	I hope so, small routines can help a lot.

Engine 115: Something From Your Culture That You're Proud Of

Det finns något i min kultur som jag är särskilt stolt över.	There's one thing in my culture that I'm especially proud of.
Jaha, vad är det?	Oh, what is it?
Hur vi värdesätter gemenskap och att hjälpa varandra.	The way we value community and helping others.
Varför är det viktigt för dig?	Why is that important to you?
För att det skapar en känsla av trygghet och tillhörighet.	Because it creates a feeling of safety and belonging.
Hur märks det i vardagen?	How does this show up in daily life?

Att ingen lämnas ensam, hjälp finns alltid när den behövs.	In the fact that no one is left alone, help is always available if needed.
En fin sak, kulturell stolthet för människor närmare varandra.	A beautiful thing, cultural pride brings people closer.
Ja, och det känns verkligen meningsfullt.	It does, and it feels very meaningful.

Engine 116: A Symbol That Represents You Right Now

Om jag skulle välja en symbol som representerar mig just nu, vet jag vad det skulle vara.	If I had to choose a symbol representing me right now, I know what it would be.
Jaha, vilken symbol är det?	Oh, what symbol is it?
En liten lykta, en som lyser precis tillräckligt framåt.	A small lantern, the kind that lights just enough of the path ahead.
Varför valde du den?	Why did you choose it?
För att jag känner att jag rör mig framåt lugnt, ett steg i taget.	Because I feel like I'm moving forward calmly, one step at a time.
Vad säger den om din situation just nu?	What does it say about your state right now?
Att jag inte har bråttom, och att ljuset räcker dit jag ska.	That I'm not in a hurry, and that the light is enough for where I need to go.
En vacker bild, den säger mycket om inre balans.	Beautiful metaphor, it says a lot about inner balance.
Så känner jag också.	I think so too.

Engine 117: Something That Motivates You When You Feel Low

När jag känner mig nere finns det något som motiverar mig.	When I feel low, there's something that motivates me.
Jaha, vad är det?	Oh, what is it?
Att gå ut och gå, även en kort promenad hjälper.	Walking outside, even a short walk clears my thoughts.
Hur hjälper det dig?	How does it help you?
Naturen lugnar mig och påminner mig om att allt rör sig framåt.	Nature calms me and reminds me things move forward even when it doesn't feel like it.
Varför ger det dig styrka?	Why does this bring strength?
För att andningen blir lugnare och tankarna öppnar sig steg för steg.	Because my breath evens out and my mind opens little by little.
Ett fint sätt att stötta dig själv.	A beautiful way to support yourself, it shows inner wisdom.
Jag tror det, även ett litet steg hjälper.	I think so, even a small step helps.

Engine 118: A Place Where You Feel Completely Safe

Det finns en plats där jag känner mig helt trygg.	There's one place where I feel completely safe.
Jaha, vilken plats är det?	Oh, what place is it?
En gammal skogsstig nära mitt barndomshem.	An old forest path near my childhood home.
Varför känner du dig trygg där?	Why do you feel safe there?
För att allt är bekant, tyst och mjukt, som om tiden stannar.	Because everything is familiar, quiet, and gentle, like time stops.

Vilka ljud eller färger hör till platsen?

What sounds or colors are connected to it?

Lövens mjuka prassel och skogens gröna ljus.

The soft rustling of leaves and the green light of the forest.

En vacker plats, känslan av trygghet är värdefull.

A beautiful place, the feeling of safety is truly precious.

Ja, jag går dit i tanken när jag behöver lugn.

It is, I go there in my mind whenever I need peace.

Engine 119: A Quality You Appreciate in Other People

Det finns en egenskap hos människor som jag verkligen uppskattar.

There's one quality in people I deeply appreciate.

Jaha, vilken egenskap?

Oh, which quality?

Äkta vänlighet, ett varmt och lugnt sätt att vara med andra.

Genuine kindness, a warm, unhurried way of being with others.

Varför tycker du om det?

Why do you like it?

För att det skapar tillit och gör världen lite mjukare.

Because it creates trust and makes the world a bit softer.

Hur känns det att vara med sådana människor?

How does it feel to be around people like that?

Lugnt, att bli sedd och uppskattad.

Calm, seen, and appreciated.

En fin insikt, det speglar dina värderingar.

A beautiful insight, it reflects your own values.

Jag tror det, vänlighet stannar kvar länge.

I think so, kindness always stays with you.

Engine 120: Something That Helps You Reset After a Stressful Day

När dagen har varit stressig har jag ett sätt som hjälper mig att återställa mig.	When I've had a stressful day, I have one method that helps me reset.
Jaha, vad är det?	Oh, what is it?
Jag lägger undan telefonen och går ut på en lugn promenad.	I put my phone away and go for an unhurried walk.
Hjälper det direkt eller gradvis?	Does it help immediately or gradually?
Gradvis, men redan efter några minuter märker jag att andningen lugnar sig.	Gradually, but after a few minutes my breathing starts to calm down.
Finns det en särskild känsla kopplad till det?	Is there a certain atmosphere connected to it?
Ja, en tyst kväll och frisk luft känns läkande.	Yes, a quiet evening and fresh air feel healing.
Ett fint sätt att återhämta sig, det viktigaste är att det ger dig lugn.	A wonderful reset method, what matters is that it brings you peace.
Ja, det hjälper varje gång.	It does, it helps every time.

Engine 121: A Habit You Want to Build Into Your Life

Jag skulle vilja bygga in en ny vana i mitt liv.	I'd like to build one new habit into my life.
Jaså, vilken vana är det?	Oh, what habit?
Morgonskrivande, några minuter för att klargöra mina tankar.	Morning journaling, a few minutes to clear my thoughts.
Varför är det viktigt för dig?	Why is it important to you?

Det hjälper mig att börja dagen lugnare.	It helps me start the day more calmly.
Vad skulle vara det minsta steget att börja?	What's the smallest step to begin?
Jag skriver bara en mening varje morgon.	I'll write just one sentence each morning.
Ett fint mål, en ny vana kan föra med sig mycket gott.	A wonderful goal, a new habit can bring a lot of good.
Jag tror det, och små steg känns möjliga.	I think so, and small steps feel doable.

Engine 122: A Memory That Always Makes You Smile

Jag har ett minne som alltid får mig att le.	I have one memory that always makes me smile.
Jaså, vilket minne är det?	Oh, what memory?
En sommardag vid sjön, vänner, skratt och en varm kväll.	A summer day by the lake, friends, laughter, and a warm evening.
Varför har det stannat kvar hos dig?	Why has it stayed with you?
För att allt i den stunden kändes lätt och äkta.	Because in that moment everything felt light and genuine.
Hur var stämningen i minnet?	What was the atmosphere like?
Mjuk, solig, som om tiden hade stannat.	Soft, sunny, as if time had stopped.
Ett underbart minne, sådana stunder är värda att bevara.	A lovely memory, moments like that are worth treasuring.
Det är de, att tänka på det gör mig alltid på gott humör.	They are, remembering it always lifts my mood.

Engine 123: Something You Hope to Experience in the Next Few Years

Jag hoppas att jag kan uppleva en särskild sak under de kommande åren.	I hope to experience one special thing in the next few years.
Jaså, vad hoppas du få uppleva?	Oh, what do you hope to experience?
Jag skulle vilja resa till en plats som jag har tänkt på sedan barndomen.	I'd like to travel to a place I've imagined since childhood.
Varför är det viktigt?	Why is it important?
För att det känns som att uppfylla en lång, stilla önskan.	Because it feels like fulfilling a long, quiet wish.
Vilka känslor väcker tanken?	What feelings does it bring?
Entusiasm, lugn och lite spänning.	Excitement, calmness, and a bit of thrill.
En vacker dröm, jag hoppas att den blir verklighet vid rätt tidpunkt.	A beautiful hope, I hope it comes true at the right time.
Jag tror det också, det ger mig något att se fram emot.	I think so too, it gives me something to look forward to.

Engine 124: A Decision That Changed You for the Better

Jag tog en gång ett beslut som förändrade mitt liv till det bättre.	I once made a decision that changed my life for the better.
Jaså, vilket beslut var det?	Oh, what decision was it?
Jag bestämde mig för att sluta med något som inte längre gynnade mitt välbefinnande.	I decided to stop something that no longer served my well-being.
Var beslutet svårt?	Was it difficult?

Ja, men jag visste inom mig att det var rätt val.	Yes, but I knew inside that it was the right choice.
Hur påverkade det din vardag?	How did it affect your daily life?
Jag kände att jag fick utrymme att andas och skapa en ny början.	I felt I gained space to breathe and create a new beginning.
En fin insikt, sådana beslut stärker oss.	A beautiful insight, decisions like that strengthen us.
Så tänker jag också.	I think so too.

Engine 125: A Feeling You Wish You Could Hold Onto Longer

Ibland känner jag något som jag önskar skulle vara längre.	Sometimes I feel something I wish would last longer.
Jaså, vilken känsla är det?	Oh, what feeling is it?
En djup ro, en sådan stilla, mjuk frid.	A deep calm, a quiet, soft stillness.
När känner du den?	When do you feel it?
Tidigt på morgonen, innan världen vaknar.	Early in the morning, before the world wakes up.
Hur känns det inom dig?	How does it feel inside you?
Som en varm andning som mjukt lugnar sinnet.	Like a warm breath that gently smooths the mind.
En vacker känsla, jag hoppas att du hittar den ofta.	A beautiful feeling, I hope you find it often.
Det hoppas jag också, den påminner mig om vem jag verkligen är.	I think so too, it reminds me of who I really am.

Engine 126: A Path You Might Have Taken in Another Version of Your Life

---

Om mitt liv hade gått lite annorlunda, kan jag föreställa mig en alternativ väg.	If my life had gone differently, I can imagine an alternate path.
Jaså, hur skulle den vägen ha varit?	Oh, what kind of path?
Jag skulle kanske ha studerat ett helt annat område, något konstnärligt.	I might have studied a completely different field, something artistic.
Var det ett realistiskt val?	Was it realistic?
Kanske, men då var jag för rädd för osäkerhet.	Perhaps, but back then I feared uncertainty too much.
Vad var det som lockade med den vägen?	What attracted you to it?
Friheten, kreativiteten och möjligheten att se världen ur en annan vinkel.	The freedom, creativity, and the chance to see the world from another angle.
En vacker reflektion, alternativa vägar avslöjar mycket om vår inre värld.	A beautiful reflection, alternate paths reveal so much about our inner world.
Det gör de, och kanske lever en del av den vägen fortfarande i mig.	They do, and maybe part of that path still lives in me.

Engine 127: Advice You Would Give to Your Younger Self

Om jag kunde tala med mitt yngre jag, skulle jag ha ett viktigt råd.	If I could talk to my younger self, I'd have one important piece of advice.
Vilket råd skulle du ge?	What advice would you give?
Jag skulle säga: "Lita mer på dig själv, du är starkare än du tror."	I would say: "Trust yourself more, you're stronger than you think."
I vilket skede av livet skulle du ha behövt detta?	At what stage of life would this have helped?

Kanske när jag var rädd för att misslyckas och väntade på andras godkännande.	Probably when I feared failure and waited for others' approval.
Varför känns detta råd viktigt nu?	Why does it feel important now?
För att jag ser hur mycket onödig tyngd jag bar med mig.	Because I see how much unnecessary weight I carried with me.
Ett vackert råd, det visar tillväxt och mildhet mot dig själv.	A beautiful piece of advice, it shows growth and gentleness toward yourself.
Det gör det, och kanske lyssnar jag äntligen på det nu.	It does, and maybe I'm finally listening to it now.

Engine 128: A Moment When You Surprised Yourself

En gång gjorde jag något som överraskade mig helt.	Once, I did something that completely surprised me.
Jaså, vad gjorde du?	Oh? What did you do?
Jag talade spontant inför en stor publik, trots att jag brukar undvika att stå i centrum.	I spoke spontaneously to a large audience, even though I usually avoid being the center of attention.
Varför överraskade det dig?	Why did it surprise you?
För att jag kände ett oväntat lugn, inte panik.	Because I felt unexpected calm, not panic.
Vad visade detta ögonblick dig?	What did this moment show you?
Kanske att jag vågar mer än jag trodde.	Maybe that I'm braver than I thought.
En vacker insikt, sådana ögonblick avslöjar inre styrka.	A beautiful insight, such moments reveal inner strength.

Ja, och det gav mig självförtroende inför framtida utmaningar.	Yes, and it gave me confidence for future challenges.

Engine 129: A Sensation or Sound That Brings You Calm

Det finns ett ljud som lugnar mig direkt.	There's a sound that calms me instantly.
Vilket ljud är det?	What sound is it?
Det lätta smattret av regn mot fönstret.	The gentle tapping of rain against the window.
När lugnar det dig som mest?	When does it calm you the most?
På kvällen, när resten av världen saktar ner.	In the evening, when the rest of the world slows down.
Hur känns det i din kropp?	How does it feel in your body?
Som en varm våg som jämnar ut min andning.	Like a warm wave that evens out my breathing.
Ett vackert ögonblick, regn kan kännas som naturens egen vaggvisa.	A beautiful moment, rain can feel like nature's lullaby.
Så sant, det påminner mig om att stanna upp.	So true, it reminds me to pause.

Engine 130: Something You've Learned to Appreciate More with Time

Det finns något som jag har lärt mig att uppskatta mer med åren.	There's something I've learned to appreciate more over the years.
Jaså, vad är det?	Oh? What is it?

Tysta stunder, de små pauserna där världen verkar andas.	Quiet moments, the small pauses where the world seems to breathe.
Uppskattade du dem mindre tidigare?	Did you appreciate them less before?
Ja, jag tyckte att de var obetydliga.	Yes, I thought they were insignificant.
Vad förändrade ditt sätt att tänka?	What changed your perspective?
Kanske hektiska år, motgångar och åldrande, de lärde mig värdet av lugn.	Maybe busy years, challenges, and aging, they taught me the value of calm.
En vacker insikt, de stunderna är livets hjärta.	A beautiful insight, those moments are the heart of life.
Ja, och nu söker jag dem medvetet.	Yes, and now I seek them intentionally.

Engine 131: A Small Act of Kindness You'll Never Forget

Jag minns en liten vänlig handling som jag aldrig kommer att glömma.	I remember one small act of kindness I'll never forget.
Vad hände?	What happened?
En främling höll upp dörren och log, just den dagen när jag kände mig helt utmattad.	A stranger held the door and smiled, on a day when I felt completely worn down.
Varför berörde det dig så mycket?	Why did it move you so much?
För att ingen visste hur svår min dag var, men ändå behandlade han mig vänligt.	Because no one knew how hard my day was, yet he treated me gently.
Hur fick det dig att känna?	How did it make you feel?
Som om någon såg mig, trots att jag inte sa ett ord.	Like someone saw me, even though I said nothing.
Ett vackert minne, vänlighet kan verkligen förändra en dag.	A beautiful memory, kindness can truly change the course of a day.

Det kan det, och jag försöker minnas det när jag möter andra.

It can, and I try to remember that when I meet others.

Engine 132: Something You Consider a Personal Strength - That You Didn't Notice at First

Jag har insett att jag har en styrka som jag inte märkte från början.

I've realized I have a strength I didn't recognize at first.

Jaså, vilken styrka är det?

Oh? What strength is it?

Förmågan att förbli lugn när det är kaos omkring mig.

The ability to stay calm when there's chaos around me.

När märkte du det?

When did you notice it?

Först när människor började förlita sig på mig i svåra stunder.

Only when people started relying on me during difficult moments.

Hur har denna styrka hjälpt dig?

How has this strength helped you?

Den ger mig klarhet och hjälper mig att fatta bättre beslut.

It gives me clarity and helps me make better decisions.

En vacker insikt, lugn är en sällsynt och värdefull gåva.

A beautiful insight, calmness is a rare and valuable gift.

Ja, och jag har lärt mig att uppskatta den hos mig själv.

Yes, and I've learned to appreciate it in myself.

Engine 133: Something You Look Forward to in the Next Chapter of Your Life

Jag ser verkligen fram emot en sak i nästa kapitel av mitt liv.

There's something I'm really looking forward to in the next chapter of my life.

Jaså, vad ser du fram emot?

Oh? What are you looking forward to?

Möjligheten att börja något helt nytt, kanske ett litet projekt eller äventyr.	The chance to begin something completely new, maybe a small project or adventure.
Varför känns det viktigt?	Why does it feel important?
För att jag vill skapa utrymme för kreativitet och lätthet.	Because I want to create space for creativity and lightness.
Hur skulle det kunna förändra ditt liv?	How might it change your life?
Genom att ge mig en ny riktning och motivation.	By giving me a new direction and motivation.
En vacker vision, jag hoppas att nästa kapitel öppnar sig för dig på rätt sätt.	A beautiful vision, I hope the next chapter unfolds for you in exactly the right way.
Jag hoppas det också, jag känner mig redo för nästa steg.	I hope so too, I feel ready for the next step.

Engine 134: A Lesson You Learned the Hard Way But Are Grateful For Now

Jag lärde mig en gång en viktig sak den svåra vägen, men jag är tacksam för det nu.	I once learned an important lesson the hard way, but I'm grateful for it now.
Jaså, vilken lärdom var det?	Oh? What lesson was it?
Att jag inte behöver behaga alla, och att gränser är en form av självrespekt.	That I don't have to please everyone, and that boundaries are a form of self-respect.
Varför var det så svårt då?	Why was it so hard back then?
För att jag var rädd att förlora människor om jag sa "nej."	Because I feared I'd lose people if I said "no."
Hur förändrade den här lärdomen dig?	How did the lesson change you?

Jag lärde mig att rätt människor stannar även när jag sätter gränser.	I learned that the right people stay even when I set boundaries.
En vacker insikt, gränser är verkligen en del av att växa.	A beautiful insight, boundaries truly are part of growth.
Och nu är jag tacksam, för det lärde mig att leva friare och starkare.	And now I'm grateful, because it taught me to live more freely and confidently.

Engine 135: A Small Daily Ritual That Makes Your Day Better

Jag har en liten daglig ritual som gör min dag bättre.	I have a small daily ritual that makes my day better.
Jaså, vad är det?	Oh? What is it?
Jag dricker min första kopp te i lugn och ro, utan telefon eller stress.	I drink my first cup of tea calmly, without my phone or any rush.
När började du med denna vana?	When did you start this habit?
Kanske för ett par år sedan, när livet kändes för hektiskt.	Maybe a couple of years ago, when life felt too hectic.
Hur känns det inom dig?	How does it feel inside you?
Som ett litet ankare, andningen lugnar sig och tankarna klarnar.	Like a small anchor, my breathing steadies and my mind clears.
Ett vackert ögonblick, sådana rutiner skapar en god rytm i livet.	A beautiful moment, routines like that create a healthy rhythm.
Ja, och det hjälper mig att börja dagen med en bättre känsla.	Yes, and it helps me begin the day with a better mindset.

Engine 136: Something Small That Always Makes You Smile

Det finns en liten sak som alltid får mig att le.	There's a small thing that always makes me smile.
Jaså, vad är det?	Oh? What is it?
När jag ser någon skratta äkta, sådant skratt smittar.	When I see someone laughing genuinely, that kind of laughter is contagious.
Varför berör det dig?	Why does it touch you?
För att det påminner mig om att glädje fortfarande finns, även när dagen är tung.	Because it reminds me that joy still exists, even on heavy days.
Hur känns det inom dig?	How does it feel inside you?
Som om mitt hjärta blir lättare för en stund.	Like my heart becomes lighter for a moment.
Ett fint ögonblick, äkta skratt är som en liten läkande kraft i vardagen.	A lovely moment, genuine laughter is like a small healing force in daily life.
Sant, och därför ler jag varje gång.	True, and that's why I smile every time.

Engine 137: Something You Believe Is Worth Protecting

Jag tror att det finns en sak som alltid är värd att skydda.	I believe there is one thing that is always worth protecting.
Vad är det?	What is it?
Ärlighet, mot sig själv och mot andra.	Honesty, with oneself and with others.
Varför är det så viktigt för dig?	Why is it so important to you?
För att utan ärlighet försvinner tilliten, och allt börjar falla isär.	Because without honesty, trust disappears, and everything begins to fall apart.
Hur visar det sig i din vardag?	How does it show up in your daily life?

Jag försöker tala rakt och leva så att min inre och yttre värld är i linje.	I try to speak directly and live so that my inner and outer worlds align.
En vacker tanke, ärlighet är ett av de djupaste värdena att skydda.	A beautiful thought, honesty is one of the most deeply worth-protecting values.
Ja, det är som en grund som allt annat byggs på.	Yes, it's like the foundation everything else is built on.

Engine 138: Something You Didn't Think You Could Do, But Eventually Did

---

Det finns något jag aldrig trodde att jag skulle klara, men jag gjorde det.	There's something I never thought I could do, but I did.
Vad gjorde du?	What did you do?
Jag höll ett tal inför en stor publik, trots att jag alltid hade varit rädd för att tala inför folk.	I gave a speech to a large audience, even though I had always feared public speaking.
Varför kändes det omöjligt?	Why did it feel impossible?
För att jag trodde att nervositeten skulle ta min röst och mina tankar.	Because I thought anxiety would steal my voice and my thoughts.
Vad fick dig att försöka?	What made you try?
Jag ville växa, och jag visste att jag måste möta min rädsla.	I wanted to grow, and I knew I had to face my fear.
Hur kändes det att lyckas?	How did it feel to succeed?
Som om jag hade öppnat en dörr till en ny värld.	Like I had opened a door into a new world.
En fantastisk berättelse, sådana ögonblick kan förändra livets riktning.	A wonderful story, moments like this can shift the direction of a life.
Ja, och nu vet jag att jag klarar mer än jag trodde.	Yes, and now I know I'm capable of more than I thought.

Engine 139: A Memory That Still Feels Vivid, Even After Many Years

Jag har ett minne som fortfarande känns levande, även efter många år.	I have a memory that still feels vivid, even after many years.
Vilket minne är det?	What memory is it?
Ögonblicket när jag såg havet för första gången som barn.	The moment I saw the ocean for the first time as a child.
Varför stannade det kvar hos dig?	Why did it stay with you?
För att det kändes gränslöst, som om världen öppnade sig framför mig.	Because it felt boundless, like the world opened in front of me.
Minns du andra detaljer?	Do you remember other details?
Ja, doften av salt, ljudet av måsar och den varma sanden under mina fötter.	Yes, the smell of salt, the sound of seagulls, the warm sand under my feet.
Ett vackert minne, sådana stunder följer oss genom hela livet.	A beautiful memory, moments like that travel with us through life.
Ja, och varje gång jag minns det känner jag samma frihet.	Yes, and whenever I remember it, I feel the same freedom.

Engine 140: A Version of Yourself You're Growing Into

Jag känner att jag växer mot en version av mig själv som jag vill vara.	I feel myself growing toward a version of me I want to be.
Hur är den versionen?	What version is it?
En lugnare, klokare person som lyssnar bättre på sig själv.	A calmer, wiser person who listens to themselves more.
Varför just den riktningen?	Why that direction?

För att jag har insett att ett långsamt, medvetet liv passar mig bättre än ständig brådska.	Because I've realized that a slow, mindful life suits me better than constant hurry.
Vad gör du redan nu för att stödja denna förändring?	What are you doing now to support this change?
Jag lär mig att säga "nej", vila mer och lyssna på min kropps signaler.	I'm learning to say "no," rest more, and listen to my body's signals.
En vacker resa, ditt framtida jag väntar på dig med öppna armar.	A beautiful journey, your future self is waiting with open arms.
Och det känns som att jag äntligen är redo att gå mot henne.	And it feels like I'm finally ready to walk toward them.

Engine 141: A Quality You Deeply Appreciate in Others

Det finns en egenskap hos människor som jag verkligen uppskattar djupt.	There's a quality in people I deeply appreciate.
Vilken egenskap är det?	What quality is it?
Äkta värme, förmågan att få någon att känna sig sedd.	Genuine warmth, the ability to make someone feel seen.
Varför är den viktig för dig?	Why is it important to you?
För att den skapar tillit och lugn, utan någon stor gest.	Because it creates trust and calm without any grand gesture.
Hur känns det när någon visar det för dig?	How does it feel when someone shows it to you?
Som att vara hemma i sin egen kropp för ett ögonblick.	Like being at home in your own body for a moment.
En vacker tanke, värme är en av de mest mänskliga egenskaperna.	A beautiful thought, warmth is one of the most human traits.

Ja, och därför värdesätter jag den i varje möte.	Yes, and that's why I value it in any interaction.

Engine 142: A Priority That Has Become Clearer to You Over Time

Med tiden har en livsprioritet blivit mycket tydligare för mig.	Over time, one life priority has become much clearer to me.
Vad är det?	What is it?
Ett lugnt, balanserat vardagsliv, inte ständig brådska.	A calm, balanced daily life, not constant rush.
Vad gjorde det så viktigt för dig?	What made it important for you?
Jag insåg att brådska tog mer från mig än den gav.	I realized that rushing took more from me than it gave.
Hur visar det sig i din vardag nu?	How does this show up in your daily life?
Jag tar fler pauser, säger oftare "nej", och prioriterar vila.	I take more breaks, say "no" more often, and prioritize rest.
En fin insikt, klarhet gör livet mer rymligt.	A wonderful insight, clarity makes life more spacious.
Ja, och det hjälper mig att leva i min egen rytm.	Yes, and it helps me live in my own rhythm.

Engine 143: A Gesture That Made You Feel Truly Understood

Det finns en gest som fick mig att känna mig verkligen förstådd.	There's a gesture that made me feel truly understood.
Vilken gest var det?	What gesture was it?

En vän lämnade ett lugnt meddelande till mig där hen sa att hen fanns där för mig, utan någon press.	A friend left me a calm message saying they were there for me, with no pressure.
Hur kändes det?	How did it feel?
Som om någon hade sagt: "Du har utrymme att vara precis som du är."	As if someone said: "You have space to be exactly as you are."
Varför betydde det så mycket för dig?	Why did it mean so much?
För att jag inte ens hade insett att jag behövde den sortens mildhet.	Because I hadn't realized I needed that kind of gentleness.
Ett vackert ögonblick, och säkert en viktig påminnelse om att du är sedd.	A beautiful moment, and surely a reminder that you are seen.
Ja, och det lärde mig också hur jag kan vara mild mot andra.	Yes, and it taught me how I can be gentle with others too.

Engine 144: A Way You See Yourself Differently Now Than Before

Jag ser mig själv annorlunda nu än tidigare.	I see myself differently now than before.
På vilket sätt?	In what way?
Jag brukade tänka att jag alltid måste vara stark. Nu ser jag att sårbarhet också är styrka.	I used to think I always had to be strong. Now I see that vulnerability is also strength.
Vad ledde till denna insikt?	What led to this realization?
Ett svårt år, jag lärde mig att lyssna bättre på mig själv.	A difficult year, I learned to listen to myself more.
Hur känns denna förändring i vardagen?	How does this change feel in daily life?

Lättare, mer äkta. Jag tvingar mig inte längre att fortsätta bortom mina gränser.	Lighter, more authentic. I no longer force myself beyond my limits.
En vacker förändring, att acceptera sig själv är ett stort steg.	A beautiful shift, self-acceptance is a major step.
Ja, och det har gjort livet lugnare.	Yes, and it has made life calmer.

Engine 145: A Boundary You've Learned to Set

Jag har lärt mig att sätta en viktig gräns i mitt liv.	I've learned to set an important boundary in my life.
Vilken gräns är det?	What boundary is it?
Jag säger numera "nej" när min tid eller energi inte räcker till.	I say "no" now when my time or energy isn't enough.
Var det svårt för dig?	Was that difficult for you?
Ja, jag brukade vara rädd för att göra människor besvikna.	Yes, I used to fear disappointing people.
Hur har denna gräns påverkat ditt liv?	How has this boundary affected your life?
Jag är lugnare och orkar mer, och ingen blev faktiskt arg.	I'm calmer and have more energy, and no one actually got angry.
En fin förändring, ibland är "nej" den största gåvan till sig själv.	A great shift, sometimes "no" is the greatest gift you can give yourself.
Ja, och det känns äntligen naturligt.	Yes, and it finally feels natural.

Engine 146: A Moment When You Were Braver Than You Realized

Det fanns ett ögonblick då jag var modigare än jag då förstod.	There was a moment when I was braver than I realized at the time.
Vilket ögonblick var det?	What moment was it?
När jag bytte jobb under osäkra tider.	When I changed jobs during uncertain times.
Hur kände du dig före beslutet?	How did you feel before the decision?
Jag var rädd för att misslyckas, men jag ville inte stanna kvar.	I feared failure, but I didn't want to stay stuck.
Varför ser du det nu som modigt?	Why do you now see it as brave?
För att jag tog en risk för en bättre framtid.	Because I took a risk for a better future.
Det är fint, mod visar sig ofta först i efterhand.	That's wonderful, courage often reveals itself afterwards.
Ja, och nu litar jag mer på mig själv.	Yes, and now I trust myself more.

Engine 147: Someone Who Helped You Grow in an Unexpected Way

Det finns en person som hjälpte mig att växa på ett oväntat sätt.	There is someone who helped me grow in an unexpected way.
Vem var det?	Who was it?
Min gamla lärare, hen såg potential i mig som jag själv inte såg.	My old teacher, they saw potential I didn't see in myself.
Vad gjorde hen som påverkade dig?	What did they do that affected you?
Hen sa: "Du har förmågan att tänka djupt. Slösa inte bort den."	They said, "You have the ability to think deeply. Don't waste it."
Varför var det så betydelsefullt?	Why was it so meaningful?

För att det fick mig att tro på mig själv på ett nytt sätt.	Because it made me believe in myself differently.
Ett vackert minne, och en stark påverkan.	A beautiful memory, and a powerful influence.
Ja, det formade hela riktningen i mitt liv.	Yes, it shaped the entire direction of my life.

Engine 148: Something You Wish You Had Realized Earlier in Life

---

Det finns något jag önskar att jag hade förstått tidigare.	There's something I wish I had understood earlier.
Vad är det?	What is it?
Att vila inte är lathet, utan nödvändigt.	That rest isn't laziness, it's essential.
Varför hade du behövt den tanken tidigare?	Why would you have needed that idea earlier?
För att jag som yngre ofta blev utmattad eftersom jag var rädd för att stanna upp.	Because when I was younger, I often burned out from fear of slowing down.
Hur känns det nu när du förstår det?	How do you feel now that you understand it?
Lugnare. Som om jag äntligen har gett mig själv tillåtelse att andas.	More peaceful. Like I've finally given myself permission to breathe.
En vacker insikt, och en viktig påminnelse.	A beautiful insight, and an important reminder.
Ja, och det förändrar mitt sätt att leva.	Yes, and it changes the way I live now.

Engine 149: Something You Haven't Done Yet but Still Want to Do

---

Det finns något jag ännu inte har gjort, men som jag fortfarande vill göra.	There's something I haven't done yet but still want to do.
Vad är det?	What is it?
Jag vill skriva klart min egen bok.	I want to finish writing my own book.
Varför är det viktigt för dig?	Why is it important to you?
För att jag känner att jag har en berättelse som vill bli berättad.	Because I feel I have a story that wants to be told.
Vad har hållit dig tillbaka?	What has held you back?
Tidsbrist, och kanske lite osäkerhet.	Lack of time, and maybe a little self-doubt.
Hur skulle det kännas att bli klar med den?	How would it feel to finish it?
Befriande. Som att ge röst åt något inom mig.	Liberating, like giving a voice to something inside me.
Ett vackert mål, och helt möjligt.	A beautiful goal, and completely possible.
Ja, jag hoppas att rätt stund kommer snart.	Yes, I hope the right moment comes soon.

Engine 150: A Lesson Life Keeps Teaching You Again and Again

Det finns en livslärdom som återkommer till mig om och om igen.	There's a life lesson that keeps returning to me.
Vilken lärdom?	What lesson?
Att jag måste stanna när min kropp säger åt mig att stanna.	That I need to stop when my body tells me to stop.
Hur upprepar det sig i ditt liv?	How does this repeat in your life?

Varje gång jag stressar för mycket tvingar något mig att sakta ner.	Whenever I rush too much, something forces me to slow down.
Varför tror du att just denna lärdom återkommer?	Why do you think this one keeps coming back?
För att jag aldrig har varit särskilt bra på att lyssna på mig själv.	Because I've never been very good at listening to myself.
Hur påverkar denna lärdom ditt sätt att leva nu?	How does this lesson affect the way you live now?
Jag skapar mer utrymme för vila och ger mig själv tillåtelse att andas.	I make more space for rest and give myself permission to breathe.
En vacker lärdom, och tydligt en viktig del av din resa.	A beautiful lesson, and clearly an important part of your journey.
Ja, och kanske lär jag mig den lite djupare den här gången.	Yes, and maybe this time I learn it a little more deeply.

Engine 151: Gently Steering a Conversation Back on Course

Innan vi fortsätter skulle jag vilja återvända till en sak för ett ögonblick.	Before we continue, I'd like to return to one thing for a moment.
Till vilken sak?	To what thing?
Till hur vi definierade hela situationen i början.	To how we defined the whole situation at the beginning.
Hur ser du på det nu?	How do you see it now?
Det känns som att det påverkar allt annat vi pratar om.	It feels like it affects everything else we're discussing.
Förstod jag rätt att du vill förtydliga utgångspunkten?	So did I understand correctly that you want to clarify the starting point?

Precis så, annars börjar samtalet falla isär.	Exactly, otherwise the conversation starts to fall apart.
Bra poäng. Det gör helheten tydligare.	Good point. This makes the whole picture clearer.
Tack, nu kan vi fortsätta naturligt.	Thanks, now we can continue naturally.
Överens, vi fortsätter härifrån.	Agreed, let's continue from here.

Engine 152: Finding Common Ground Through Humor

Det här är kanske inte en särskilt vetenskaplig observation, men…	This may not be a very scientific observation, but…
Berätta bara.	Go on.
Jag märker ofta att jag förstår saker först i efterhand.	I often notice I only understand things afterward.
Det låter bekant.	That sounds familiar.
Det är oftast då jag skrattar lite åt mig själv.	This is usually the point where I laugh a little at myself.
Det är nog ganska hälsosamt.	That's probably quite healthy.
Det tycker jag också.	That's what I think too.
Lite humor hjälper att acceptera det.	A little humor helps to accept it.
Åtminstone kan man lära sig något av det.	At least we can learn something from this.
Och gå vidare lite lättare.	And move forward a little more lightly.

Engine 153: Repairing a Misstep with Grace and Humor

Vänta lite, det där kom inte riktigt ut rätt.	Wait a moment, that didn't come out quite right.
Hur menar du?	How so?
Jag menade det mer som en observation än som kritik.	I meant this more as an observation than a criticism.
Aha, nu förstår jag bättre.	Ah, I understand better now.
Jag uttryckte mig lite klumpigt.	I said that a bit awkwardly.
Ingen fara, sånt händer.	No worries, it happens.
Ibland springer språket före tanken.	Sometimes language runs ahead of thought.
Det är väldigt mänskligt.	That's very human.
Tack för ditt tålamod.	Thanks for your patience.
Självklart, vi fortsätter härifrån.	Of course, let's continue from here.

Engine 154: Redirecting the Conversation Without Creating Friction

Det här är verkligen intressant.	This is definitely interesting.
Ja, det finns mycket att prata om här.	It is, there's plenty to discuss here.
Skulle vi ändå kunna återgå till den ursprungliga frågan?	Could we return to the original question, though?
Sant, annars tappar vi lätt bort oss.	True, otherwise we'll easily get lost.
Det här är ett sådant ämne som aldrig tar slut av sig självt.	This is one of those topics that doesn't end on its own.
Bra poäng.	Good point.
Låt oss fortsätta ur det här perspektivet.	Let's continue from this perspective for now.

Överens.	Agreed.
Vi kan återkomma till det senare om det finns tid.	We can come back to this later if there's time.
Det låter bra.	Sounds good.

Engine 155: Pausing with Confidence Before Moving Forward

Här skulle jag vilja stanna upp en stund.	At this point, I'd like to pause for a moment.
Varför just nu?	Why right now?
Det här är ingen enkel fråga.	This isn't a simple question.
Ja, den har många sidor.	Yes, there are many sides to it.
Ibland kommer förståelsen först efter en stund.	Sometimes understanding comes with a delay.
Det är sant.	That's true.
Kanske är det klokt att låta det landa.	Maybe it's wise to let this settle.
Jag håller med.	I agree.
Vi återvänder till det när tankarna har klarnat.	Let's return to this when our thoughts have cleared.
Överens.	Agreed.

Engine 156: Naming the Direction of the Conversation

Kanske skulle vi en stund kunna prata om vart den här diskussionen är på väg.	Maybe we could talk for a moment about where this conversation is going.
Vad menar du?	What do you mean?

Jag känner att vi rör vid något väsentligt.	I feel like we're touching on something essential.
Ja, det finns något viktigt här.	Yes, there's something important here.
När riktningen är tydlig hittar orden lättare sin plats.	When the direction is clear, words find their place more easily.
Det låter rimligt.	That makes sense.
Det här handlar inte om att styra, utan om gemensam förståelse.	This isn't about control, but shared understanding.
Jag håller med.	I agree.
Bra, låt oss fortsätta medvetet härifrån.	Good, let's continue from here consciously.
Vi går vidare.	Let's move forward.

Engine 157: Summarizing Meaning Before Moving On

Innan vi fortsätter vill jag sammanfatta detta.	Before we continue, I'd like to pull this together.
Vad menar du?	What do you mean?
Flera viktiga saker har kommit fram här.	Several important points have come up here.
Ja, ganska många.	Yes, quite a lot.
Det handlar inte om enskilda ord, utan om helheten.	This isn't about individual words, but about the whole.
Jag förstår.	I understand.
Det här känns mer som en riktning än ett svar.	This feels more like a direction than an answer.
Det beskriver det väl.	That describes it well.

Bra, nu är det tydligare.	Good, this is clearer now.
Vi kan gå vidare härifrån.	We can move forward from here.

Engine 158: Staying with Ambiguity Without Forcing an Answer

Just nu är sakerna ännu inte helt klara.	At this point, things aren't fully clear yet.
Det känns lite obekvämt.	It feels a bit uncomfortable.
Ja, men kanske är det okej.	Yes, but maybe that's okay.
Allt behöver inte lösas direkt.	Not everything needs to be resolved immediately.
Osäkerhet betyder inte alltid att något är fel.	Uncertainty doesn't always mean something is wrong.
Det är tröstande att tänka så.	That's comforting to think about.
Vi kan återkomma till detta när det klarnar.	We can return to this when things become clearer.
Låt oss göra så.	Let's agree on that.
För nu räcker det att vi ser det.	For now, it's enough that we recognize this.
Vi fortsätter framåt.	Let's move forward.

Engine 159: Disagreeing Without Creating Opposition

Jag förstår ditt perspektiv, men jag ser det lite annorlunda.	I understand your perspective, but I see this a bit differently.
Hur då?	How so?

Det väcker en något annorlunda tolkning hos mig.	This brings up a slightly different interpretation for me.
Berätta mer.	Tell me more.
Skillnad behöver inte innebära konflikt.	Difference doesn't necessarily mean conflict.
Det är en bra påminnelse.	That's a good reminder.
Det här motsäger inte ditt tänkande, det kompletterar det.	This doesn't negate your thinking, it complements it.
Jag förstår bättre nu.	I understand better now.
Jag uppskattar att vi kan tänka olika.	I appreciate that we can think differently.
Detsamma.	Likewise.

Engine 160: Setting a Clear Boundary While Staying Warm

Här behöver jag vara tydlig med detta.	At this point, I need to be clear about this.
Vad menar du?	What do you mean?
Det här är en viktig gräns för mig.	This is an important boundary for me.
Jag förstår.	I understand.
En gräns är inte ett avvisande, det är tydlighet.	A boundary isn't rejection, it's clarity.
Det hjälper att förstå det.	That helps clarify it.
Det här stänger inte samtalet, det gör det tryggare.	This doesn't close the conversation, it makes it safer.
Jag uppskattar att du säger det så här.	I appreciate you saying this this way.
Tack för att du lyssnade.	Thank you for hearing me out.

Vi går vidare härifrån.	Let's move forward.

Engine 161: Reframing a Situation Without Dismissing Feelings

---

Jag förstår att det här känns tungt.	I understand that this feels heavy.
Det gör det verkligen.	Yes, it really does.
Det finns tydligt mycket känslor i det här.	There are clearly a lot of emotions involved here.
Det gör det, och det gör det här svårt.	There are, and it makes this difficult.
Skulle vi också kunna se på detta från ett annat perspektiv?	Could we also look at this from another perspective?
Kanske, så länge det inte tar bort känslorna.	Maybe, as long as it doesn't take the feelings away.
Det gör inte din upplevelse mindre verklig.	This doesn't make your experience any less real.
Det är skönt att höra.	That helps to hear.
Nu känns helheten lite mer öppen.	Now the whole feels a bit more open.
Låt oss fortsätta härifrån.	Let's continue from here.

Engine 162: Letting Silence Create Space for the Other Person

---

Vi kan vara här i tystnad en stund.	We can sit here quietly for a moment.
…	…
Du behöver inte svara direkt.	You don't need to answer right away.
Det hjälper.	That helps.

Tystnad är också en del av samtalet.	Silence is also part of the conversation.
Det är det.	It is.
Vad kommer upp för dig nu?	What comes to mind for you now?
Jag tror att jag börjar förstå något.	I think I'm starting to understand something.
Tack för att du delade detta.	Thank you for sharing this.
Låt oss fortsätta härifrån.	Let's continue from here.

Engine 163: Asking the Question That Changes the Frame

Får jag ställa en lite annorlunda fråga?	May I ask you one slightly different question?
Självklart.	Of course.
Vad är viktigast för dig i det här?	What matters most to you here?
Jag har inte tänkt på det så.	I haven't thought about it that way.
Du behöver inte svara direkt.	You don't need to answer right away.
Men det känns betydelsefullt.	But it feels meaningful.
Sådana frågor flyttar fokus från reaktion till intention.	Questions like this shift focus from reaction to intention.
Ja, nu ser jag det här annorlunda.	Yes, I see this differently now.
Vi kan låta den här frågan följa med oss.	We can let this question travel with us.
Låt oss fortsätta härifrån.	Let's continue from here.

Engine 164: Accepting What You Can't Control

Jag kan inte påverka allt i den här situationen.	I can't influence everything in this situation.
Det kan vara frustrerande.	That can be frustrating.
Ja, men vad kan jag fortfarande påverka?	Yes, but what can I still influence?
Kanske din egen reaktion.	Maybe your own reaction.
Även om jag inte kan kontrollera situationen kan jag kontrollera hur jag möter den.	Even if I can't control the situation, I can control how I meet it.
Det ger styrka.	That gives strength.
Min respons säger mer om mig än om omständigheterna.	My response says more about me than the circumstances.
Jag förstår bättre nu.	I understand better now.
Nu vet jag vad jag ska fokusera på.	Now I know what to focus on.
Fortsätt därifrån.	Continue from there.

Engine 165: Choosing Meaning Even When Outcomes Are Uncertain

Jag vet inte hur det här kommer att sluta.	I don't know how this will ultimately turn out.
Det kan kännas osäkert.	That can feel uncertain.
Ja, men jag känner ändå att det här har betydelse.	Yes, but I still feel that this has meaning.
Vad gör det meningsfullt?	What makes it meaningful?
Att jag handlar i linje med mina värderingar.	That I'm acting in line with my values.
Även om resultatet inte är säkert?	Even if the outcome isn't certain?

Just därför.	Precisely because of that.
Meningen kommer inte alltid från resultatet.	Meaning doesn't always come from the outcome.
Jag förstår.	I understand.
Jag fortsätter härifrån.	I'll continue from here.

Engine 166: Acting with Integrity When No One Is Watching

Ingen kanske märker vad jag gör i den här situationen.	No one may notice what I do in this situation.
Men du märker det.	But you notice.
Ja, och det räcker.	Yes, and that's enough.
Hur vill du agera?	How do you want to act?
På ett sätt som jag kan leva med senare.	In a way I can live with later.
Det låter ärligt.	That sounds honest.
Integritet behöver inte alltid en publik.	Integrity doesn't always need an audience.
Sant.	True.
Det här känns rätt för mig.	This feels right to me.
Fortsätt därifrån.	Continue from there.

Engine 167: Letting Go of Being Right to Stay Truthful

Jag behöver inte ha rätt här.	I don't need to be right here.
Vad menar du med det?	What do you mean by that?

Att ärlighet är viktigare än att vinna.	That honesty matters more than winning.
Det förändrar dynamiken.	That changes the dynamic.
Att ha rätt kan stänga dörrar.	Being right can close doors.
Och ärlighet kan öppna dem.	And honesty can open them.
Det här handlar inte om att vinna.	This isn't about winning.
Utan om att förstå.	But about understanding.
Nu känns samtalet lättare.	Now the conversation feels easier.
Låt oss fortsätta härifrån.	Let's continue from here.

Engine 168: Choosing Silence as a Conscious Response

Jag vet vad jag skulle kunna säga nu.	I know what I could say right now.
Tänker du säga det?	Are you going to say it?
Kanske inte än.	Maybe not yet.
Varför inte?	Why not?
För att rätt ögonblick inte är nu.	Because the right moment isn't now.
Det kräver tålamod.	That takes restraint.
Tystnad är inte tillbakadragande, det är ett val.	Silence isn't withdrawal, it's a choice.
Jag förstår.	I understand.
Jag är här, även om jag inte talar.	I'm here, even if I'm not speaking.
Vi fortsätter senare.	Let's continue later.

Engine 169: Knowing When a Conversation Has Done Its Work

Det känns som att den här samtalet har gjort sitt.	It feels to me like this conversation has done its work.
Jag känner likadant.	I feel that way too.
Vi har kanske sagt det som behövdes just nu.	We may have said what was needed for now.
Ja, det finns ingen anledning att pressa fram mer.	Yes, there's no need to force more.
Det här är inte ett slut, utan en mellanfas.	This isn't an endpoint, but an in-between stage.
Det känns tröstande.	That feels comforting.
Tack för det här samtalet.	Thank you for this conversation.
Tack själv.	Thank you as well.
Låt oss låta det vara här.	Let's let this be here.
Överens.	Agreed.

Engine 170: Choosing the Next Step Without Urgency

Nästa steg finns i mitt sinne, men det behöver inte ske direkt.	The next step is on my mind, but it doesn't need to happen right away.
Vilket steg är det?	What step is that?
Ett som känns naturligt och inte framtvingat.	One that feels natural, not forced.
Det låter klokt.	That sounds sensible.

Det viktiga är riktningen, inte hastigheten.	What matters is direction, not speed.
Så tänker jag också.	That's how I see it too.
Det här räcker som nästa steg.	This is enough for the next step.
Bra.	Good.
Låt oss gå vidare lugnt.	Let's move forward calmly.
Överens.	Agreed.

Engine 171: Acting Without Needing Recognition

Jag gör inte detta för att få beröm.	I'm not doing this to receive praise.
Varför gör du det då?	Then why do it?
För att det är i linje med mina värderingar.	Because it aligns with my values.
Och om ingen märker det?	What if no one notices?
Då är det fortfarande rätt.	Then it's still right.
Det kräver inre trygghet.	That takes inner certainty.
Värderingar behöver ingen publik.	Values don't need an audience.
Sant.	True.
Det räcker för mig.	This is enough for me.
Fortsätt därifrån.	Continue from there.

Engine 172: Remaining Steady When Results Are Delayed

Resultaten syns ännu inte.	The results aren't visible yet.
Det kan vara frustrerande.	That can be frustrating.

Ja, men jag vet att jag är på rätt väg.	Yes, but I know I'm on the right path.
Vad får dig att lita på det?	What makes you trust that?
Att jag fortfarande gör rätt saker.	That I'm still doing the right things.
Även om belöningen dröjer?	Even if the reward is delayed?
Tålamod är inte passivitet.	Patience isn't inactivity.
Det kräver styrka.	It takes strength.
Jag fortsätter steg för steg.	I'll keep going step by step.
Det räcker för nu.	That's enough for now.

Engine 173: Staying Aligned When Motivation Fades

Jag känner mig inte särskilt motiverad just nu.	I don't feel particularly motivated right now.
Måste du ändå fortsätta?	Do you still have to continue?
Ja, eftersom det här är i linje med mina värderingar.	Yes, because this aligns with my values.
Och om känslan inte förändras?	What if the feeling doesn't change?
Värderingar försvinner inte med känslor.	Values don't disappear with feelings.
Det låter stabilt.	That sounds steady.
Disciplin är inte hårdhet utan trohet.	Discipline isn't harshness, it's loyalty.
Jag förstår nu.	I understand now.
Det här räcker för idag.	This is enough for today.
Fortsätt därifrån.	Continue from there.

Engine 174: Choosing Consistency Over Intensity

Jag behöver inte en stor ansträngning just nu.	I don't need a big push right now.
Vad behöver du då?	What do you need then?
Konsekvens.	Consistency.
Inte intensitet?	Not intensity?
Intensitet tröttar ut, konsekvens bygger upp.	Intensity exhausts; consistency builds.
Det låter hållbart.	That sounds sustainable.
En liten men återkommande handling räcker.	A small but repeated action is enough.
Jag förstår.	I understand.
Jag väljer hellre den här takten.	I choose this pace instead.
Fortsätt därifrån.	Continue from there.

Engine 175: Continuing When No One Is Watching Anymore

Den första entusiasmen är redan borta.	The initial excitement is already over.
Hur känns det?	How does that feel?
Tyst, men klart.	Quiet, but clear.
Varför fortsätter du ändå?	Why continue anyway?
För att meningen inte försvann med entusiasmen.	Because the meaning didn't disappear with the excitement.
Det kräver uthållighet.	That takes perseverance.
När nyheten försvinner, finns meningen kvar.	When novelty fades, meaning remains.

Jag förstår.	I understand.
Det räcker som skäl att fortsätta.	That's reason enough to continue.
Fortsätt därifrån.	Continue from there.

Engine 176: Remaining Open to Learning Even After Mastery

Jag har redan lärt mig mycket här.	I've already learned a lot here.
Känns det färdigt?	Does it feel complete?
Nej, mer öppet.	No, more like open.
Hur då?	How so?
Det finns fortfarande något att lära.	There's still something to learn here.
Det kräver ödmjukhet.	That takes humility.
Verklig kunskap stänger inte nyfikenheten.	True expertise doesn't close curiosity.
Det är en bra påminnelse.	That's a good reminder.
Jag vill bevara den här öppenheten.	I want to preserve this openness.
Fortsätt därifrån.	Continue from there.

Engine 177: Releasing Certainty to Stay Adaptable

Jag är inte längre helt säker på att detta är det enda rätta sättet.	I'm no longer fully sure this is the only right way.
Är det något dåligt?	Is that a bad thing?
Nej, det ger utrymme att anpassa sig.	No, it gives room to adapt.
Och om förändringen leder dig fel?	What if change leads you astray?

Flexibilitet kan skydda det som verkligen är viktigt.	Flexibility can protect what truly matters.
Det låter klokt.	That sounds wise.
Det här är inte att ge upp, utan att förfina.	This isn't giving up; it's refining.
Jag förstår.	I understand.
Jag fortsätter härifrån med flexibilitet.	I'll continue from here with flexibility.
Fortsätt därifrån.	Continue from there.

Engine 178: Choosing Clarity Over Comfort

Det här är inte det lättaste att säga.	This isn't the easiest thing to say.
Vad menar du?	What do you mean?
Jag vill vara så tydlig som möjligt här.	I want to be as clear as possible here.
Jag uppskattar det.	I appreciate that.
Tydlighet betyder inte hårdhet.	Clarity doesn't mean harshness.
Det känns lugnande.	That's reassuring.
Otydlighet kan göra mer ont än sanningen.	Uncertainty can hurt more than truth.
Ja, det är sant.	Yes, that's true.
Nu är saker tydligare.	Now things are clearer.
Låt oss fortsätta härifrån.	Let's continue from here.

Engine 179: Standing by a Decision Even When It's Uncomfortable

---

Det här beslutet känns inte lätt.	This decision doesn't feel easy.
Varför gör du det ändå?	Why do it anyway?
För att det känns rätt, även om det är obekvämt.	Because it feels right, even though it's uncomfortable.
Och om det möter motstånd?	What if it meets resistance?
Obehag betyder inte alltid att det är fel.	Discomfort doesn't always mean a mistake.
Det är sant.	That's true.
Jag kan vara öppen för diskussion utan att backa.	I can be open to discussion without backing down.
Det låter balanserat.	That sounds balanced.
Jag står fast vid detta beslut.	I stand by this decision.
Låt oss fortsätta därifrån.	Let's continue from there.

Engine 180: Accepting Trade-offs Without Regret

Jag vet att detta val också innebär förluster.	I know this choice also comes with losses.
Är det svårt för dig?	Is that hard for you?
Ja, men det är en del av det.	Yes, but it's part of it.
Vad hjälper dig att acceptera det?	What helps you accept that?
Att det var ett medvetet val.	That this was a conscious choice.
Utan ånger?	Without regret?
Ja, jag accepterar denna avvägning.	Yes, I accept this trade-off.
Det låter moget.	That sounds mature.
Jag bär inte detta som ånger.	I won't carry this as regret.

Fortsätt därifrån.	Continue from there.

Engine 181: Holding Responsibility Without Self-Judgment

Detta är mitt ansvar.	This is my responsibility.
Känns det tungt?	Does that feel heavy?
Nej, det känns tydligt.	No, it feels clear.
Hur undviker du att klandra dig själv?	How do you avoid blaming yourself?
Genom att minnas att ansvar inte kräver skam.	By remembering responsibility doesn't require shame.
Det låter hälsosamt.	That sounds healthy.
Jag gör de nödvändiga justeringarna.	I'll make the necessary corrections.
Och går vidare?	And move forward?
Ja, klokare.	Yes, wiser.
Fortsätt därifrån.	Continue from there.

Engine 182: Letting Go of Control While Staying Responsible

Jag kan inte kontrollera allt i den här situationen.	I can't control everything in this situation.
Känns det osäkert?	Does that feel uncertain?
Ja, men också befriande.	Yes, but also freeing.
Hur förblir du ändå ansvarstagande?	How do you stay responsible then?
Jag vet vad jag ansvarar för — och vad jag inte gör.	I know what I'm responsible for — and what I'm not.

Det kräver tillit.	That takes trust.
Tillit är ett aktivt val.	Trust is an active choice.
Jag förstår.	I understand.
Jag väljer tillit här.	I choose trust here.
Fortsätt därifrån.	Continue from there.

Engine 183: Staying Grounded When Others Project Expectations Onto You

---

Jag märker att många förväntningar riktas mot mig.	I notice there are many expectations placed on me.
Känns det tungt?	Does it feel heavy?
Ibland, men nu ser jag skillnaden.	Sometimes, but now I notice the difference.
Vilken skillnad?	What difference?
Alla förväntningar är inte mina att bära.	Not all expectations are mine to carry.
Det kräver gränser.	That requires boundaries.
Gränser är inte avvisande — de är tydlighet.	Boundaries aren't rejection — they're clarity.
Det känns lugnande.	That feels calming.
Jag står kvar i mig själv här.	I stay in my own place here.
Fortsätt därifrån.	Continue from there.

Engine 184: Saying No Without Guilt

Här behöver jag säga nej.	At this point, I need to say no.

Varför?	Why?
För att det här inte är rätt val för mig just nu.	Because this isn't the right choice for me right now.
Känns det inte dåligt?	Doesn't that feel bad?
Att säga nej är också att ta ansvar.	Saying no is also taking responsibility.
Och skuldkänslan?	What about guilt?
Skuld behövs inte för en tydlig gräns.	Guilt isn't required for a clear boundary.
Jag förstår.	I understand.
Det här beslutet känns rätt för mig.	This decision feels right to me.
Fortsätt därifrån.	Continue from there.

Engine 185: Ending a Role or Chapter Without Bitterness

Den här fasen i mitt liv går mot sitt slut.	This phase in my life is coming to an end.
Hur känns det?	How does that feel?
Vemodigt, men rätt.	Bittersweet, but right.
Är det svårt att släppa taget?	Is it hard to let go?
Lite, men jag vill inte bära med mig bitterhet.	A little, but I don't want to carry bitterness.
Vad tar du med dig härifrån?	What do you take with you from this?
Lärdomarna och erfarenheterna.	The lessons and experiences.
Det låter hälsosamt.	That sounds healthy.
Jag tackar den här fasen för vad den gav mig.	I thank this phase for what it gave me.
Fortsätt därifrån.	Continue from there.

Engine 186: Beginning Again Without Discarding the Past

Jag börjar något nytt här.	I'm beginning something new here.
Känns det som en nystart?	Does it feel like a clean start?
Inte helt — mer som en fortsättning.	Not completely — more like a continuation.
Hur då?	How so?
Jag börjar inte från noll.	I'm not starting from zero.
Det ger trygghet.	That brings confidence.
Erfarenhet ger den här början djup.	Experience gives this beginning depth.
Jag förstår.	I understand.
Den här nya starten känns stabil.	This new beginning feels steady.
Fortsätt därifrån.	Continue from there.

Engine 187: Holding Hope Without Illusion

Jag hoppas att saker utvecklas i en bättre riktning.	I hope things move in a better direction.
Är det realistiskt?	Is that realistic?
Ja, eftersom jag inte bygger det på önsketänkande.	Yes, because I'm not basing it on wishes alone.
På vad då?	Then on what?
På det jag ser och kan påverka.	On what I can see and influence.
Det låter stabilt.	That sounds steady.
Verkligt hopp klarar också osäkerhet.	Real hope can withstand uncertainty.

Jag förstår.	I understand.
Jag bär med mig hoppet, men står med fötterna på jorden.	I carry hope with me, with my feet on the ground.
Fortsätt därifrån.	Continue from there.

Engine 188: Choosing Peace Over Being Right

Den här gången är fred viktigare för mig än att ha rätt.	This time, peace matters more to me than being right.
Vill du inte försvara din ståndpunkt?	Don't you want to defend your position?
Inte just nu.	Not right now.
Varför inte?	Why not?
För att den här diskussionen inte behöver en vinnare.	Because this conversation doesn't need a winner.
Det är överraskande.	That's surprising.
Samhörighet kan vara viktigare än att ha rätt.	Connection can matter more than being right.
Jag förstår.	I understand.
Jag väljer fred i detta ögonblick.	I choose peace in this moment.
Fortsätt därifrån.	Continue from there.

Engine 189: Accepting Ambiguity Without Anxiety

Allt är inte klart i den här situationen.	Not everything is clear in this situation.
Känns det obekvämt?	Does that feel uncomfortable?
Lite, men inte skrämmande.	A little, but not frightening.

Hur förblir du lugn?	How do you stay calm?
Genom att minnas att osäkerhet inte är farlig.	By remembering uncertainty isn't dangerous.
Det kräver övning.	That takes practice.
Förmågan att tåla otydlighet är ett tecken på mognad.	The ability to tolerate ambiguity is a sign of maturity.
Jag förstår.	I understand.
Jag kan vara här utan svar.	I can be here without answers.
Fortsätt därifrån.	Continue from there.

Engine 190: Living With Integrity When No Rulebook Applies

I den här situationen finns det ingen tydlig regel.	There's no clear rule for this situation.
Hur bestämmer du då?	How do you decide then?
Genom att lita på det som känns ärligt.	By trusting what feels honest.
Och om du tvivlar på dig själv?	What if you doubt yourself?
Jag minns vilka värderingar som vägleder mig.	I remember which values guide me.
Det kräver mod.	That takes courage.
En inre kompass är viktigast i oklara situationer.	An inner compass matters most in unclear situations.
Jag förstår.	I understand.
Jag står bakom detta val.	I stand behind this choice.
Fortsätt därifrån.	Continue from there.

Engine 191: Choosing Meaning Over Ease

Det här är inte det enklaste alternativet.	This isn't the easiest option.
Varför väljer du inte det enklare?	Why not choose the easier one?
För att det inte känns meningsfullt.	Because it doesn't feel meaningful.
Och ansträngningen?	What about the effort?
Jag är villig att göra arbetet.	I'm willing to do the work.
Det kräver engagemang.	That takes commitment.
Meningsfulla saker kräver ofta mer.	Meaningful things often demand more.
Jag förstår.	I understand.
Jag väljer detta medvetet.	I choose this consciously.
Fortsätt därifrån.	Continue from there.

Engine 192: Staying Kind Without Being Naïve

Jag vill vara vänlig i den här situationen.	I want to be kind in this situation.
Och om du blir utnyttjad?	What if you're taken advantage of?
Därför behöver jag också omdöme.	That's why I also need discernment.
Kan man vara vänlig och samtidigt noggrann?	Can kindness be discerning too?
Ja — annars håller det inte.	Yes — otherwise it doesn't last.
Det låter klokt.	That sounds wise.
Äkta vänlighet blundar inte.	Genuine kindness doesn't close its eyes.

Jag förstår.	I understand.
Jag väljer vänlighet som också är vis.	I choose kindness that is also wise.
Fortsätt därifrån.	Continue from there.

Engine 193: Acting With Courage Even When Fear Remains

Det här skrämmer mig.	This scares me.
Tänker du ändå agera?	Are you still going to act?
Ja.	Yes.
Hur är det möjligt?	How is that possible?
Mod kräver inte orädsla.	Courage doesn't require fearlessness.
Så rädslan stoppar dig inte?	So fear doesn't stop you?
Nej — den följer med.	No — it comes along.
Det kräver styrka.	That takes strength.
Det här räcker som mod för idag.	This is enough courage for today.
Fortsätt därifrån.	Continue from there.

Engine 194: Letting Success Change You Without Losing Yourself

---

Det här har gått bättre än jag förväntade mig.	This has gone better than I expected.
Hur känns det?	How does that feel?
Bra — och lite förvirrande.	Good — and a bit disorienting.

Varför förvirrande?	Why disorienting?
För att jag inte vill tappa bort mig själv i det.	Because I don't want to lose myself in it.
Det kräver medvetenhet.	That takes awareness.
Framgång kan stärka eller sudda ut identitet.	Success can strengthen or blur identity.
Jag förstår.	I understand.
Jag låter framgång förändra mig, men inte utplåna mig.	I'll let success change me, but not erase me.
Fortsätt därifrån.	Continue from there.

Engine 195: Handling Influence Responsibly

Jag märker att mina ord påverkar andra.	I notice that my words influence others.
Känns det bra?	Does that feel good?
Både bra och allvarligt.	Both good and serious.
Varför allvarligt?	Why serious?
För att jag inte vill styra för mycket.	Because I don't want to steer too much.
Det kräver självkontroll.	That takes self-restraint.
Verklig auktoritet tvingar inte.	True authority doesn't coerce.
Jag förstår.	I understand.
Jag använder mitt inflytande med omsorg.	I use influence with care.
Fortsätt därifrån.	Continue from there.

Engine 196: Staying Curious Rather Than Cynical

Jag har sett och upplevt mycket.	I've seen and experienced a lot.
Har det gjort dig försiktig?	Has that made you cautious?
Ja, men jag vill inte bli cynisk.	Yes, but I don't want to become cynical.
Vad väljer du istället?	What do you choose instead?
Nyfikenhet.	Curiosity.
Är inte det riskabelt?	Isn't that risky?
Cynism stänger lärandet.	Cynicism shuts down learning.
Jag förstår.	I understand.
Jag väljer nyfikenhet här.	I choose curiosity here.
Fortsätt därifrån.	Continue from there.

Engine 197: Listening More Than Speaking

Idag vill jag lyssna mer än jag talar.	Today, I want to listen more than speak.
Varför just nu?	Why now?
För att förståelse behöver utrymme.	Because understanding needs space.
Är inte tystnad obekväm?	Isn't silence awkward?
Inte om man låter den vara.	Not if you allow it.
Vad lärde du dig av att lyssna?	What did you learn by listening?
Saker jag inte hade hört om jag talat.	Things I wouldn't have heard if I'd spoken.
Det låter värdefullt.	That sounds valuable.
Jag är glad att jag lyssnade.	I'm glad I listened.

Fortsätt därifrån.	Continue from there.

Engine 198: Knowing When to Speak

Jag har varit tyst fram till nu.	I've been quiet up to this point.
Varför talar du nu?	Why speak now?
För att detta ögonblick känns rätt.	Because this moment feels right.
Hur vet du det?	How do you know?
För att orden inte längre känns stressade.	Because the words no longer feel rushed.
Det låter genomtänkt.	That sounds considered.
Visdom visar sig i när vi talar.	Wisdom shows in when we speak.
Jag förstår.	I understand.
Jag litar på denna timing.	I trust this timing.
Fortsätt därifrån.	Continue from there.

Engine 199: Letting Silence Speak

I detta ögonblick känns tystnaden rätt.	In this moment, silence feels right.
Vill du inte säga något?	Don't you want to say anything?
Inte just nu.	Not right now.
Varför inte?	Why not?
För att allt som behövs redan finns här.	Because everything needed is already here.
Det känns lugnt.	That feels calm.

Tystnad är inte tomhet.	Silence isn't emptiness.
Jag förstår.	I understand.
Den här tystnaden räcker.	This silence is enough.
Fortsätt därifrån.	Continue from there.

Engine 200: Ending Without Closure

Detta slutar inte med en tydlig slutsats.	This doesn't end with a clear conclusion.
Stör det dig?	Does that bother you?
Nej.	No.
Varför inte?	Why not?
För att allt inte behöver avslutas.	Because not everything needs to close.
Vad är det då?	Then what is this?
Ett tillräckligt slut.	A sufficient ending.
Och samtidigt?	And at the same time?
En början.	A beginning.
Ja.	Yes.

Engine 201: Recognizing Meaning Patterns

Swedish Noun Basics (en vs ett)

Type	Example	English
en-word (common gender)	en bok	a book
ett-word (neuter gender)	ett hus	a house

~80% of nouns are **en**
~20% are **ett**

Definite Forms (the noun)

Indefinite	Definite	English
en bok	boken	the book
ett hus	huset	the house

Swedish adds endings instead of "the"

Plural Examples

Singular	Plural	English
en bok	böcker	books
ett hus	hus	houses

Simple Patterns to Notice

Swedish Pattern	English Pattern
Det är en {noun}.	It is a {noun}.
Det är ett {noun}.	It is a {noun}.
{noun}-en är {adj}.	The {noun} is {adj}.
Jag har en {noun}.	I have a {noun}.
Jag ser ett {noun}.	I see a {noun}.

Mini Dialog: en / ett in Action

Swedish	English
Jag har en bok.	I have a book.
Är det en bra bok?	Is it a good book?
Ja, boken är mycket intressant.	Yes, the book is very interesting.

Swedish	English
Har du ett hus också?	Do you also have a house?
Ja, huset är stort.	Yes, the house is big.
Var ligger huset?	Where is the house located?
Det ligger nära staden.	It is near the city.
Det låter fint.	That sounds nice.
Tack!	Thanks!
Varsågod.	You're welcome.

Quick Recognition Tips

Most living things → **en**

- en hund (dog)
- en människa (person)

Many objects → **en**

- en bil (car)
- en stol (chair)

Many abstract / neutral objects → **ett**

- ett bord (table)
- ett barn (child)
- ett problem (problem)

Part 1: en / ett Review (Quick Anchor)

Type	Example	English
en-word	en stor bil	a big car
ett-word	ett stort hus	a big house

Part 2: Adjective Agreement (CORE RULE)

Adjectives change based on the noun

Form	Swedish	English
en-word	en stor bil	a big car
ett-word	ett stort hus	a big house
plural	stora bilar	big cars

Pattern Summary

Case	Pattern
en	en + adj (base form) + noun
ett	ett + adj + **-t** + noun
plural	adj + **-a** + noun

Examples

Swedish	English
en liten katt	a small cat
ett litet barn	a small child
små katter	small cats

Swedish	English
en gammal bok	an old book
ett gammalt hus	an old house
gamla böcker	old books

Part 3: Definite Forms (IMPORTANT)

When using **"the"**, adjectives always take **-a**

Swedish	**English**
den stora bilen	the big car
det stora huset	the big house
de stora bilarna	the big cars

Pattern

den/det/de + adj (-a) + noun (definite)

Part 4: Mini Dialog (Integrated Usage)

Jag ser en stor hund.	I see a big dog.
Är det en snäll hund?	Is it a kind dog?
Ja, den är väldigt snäll.	Yes, it is very kind.
Har du ett stort hus?	Do you have a big house?
Nej, jag har ett litet hus.	No, I have a small house.
Är det nya huset fint?	Is the new house nice?
Ja, det nya huset är mycket fint.	Yes, the new house is very nice.
Har du många stora rum?	Do you have many big rooms?
Ja, rummen är stora och ljusa.	Yes, the rooms are big and bright.
Det låter perfekt.	That sounds perfect.

Part 5: Quick Rules (Memorization Layer)

Rule 1: en → no change
Rule 2: ett → add **-t**
Rule 3: plural → add **-a**
Rule 4: definite → ALWAYS **-a**

Part 6: High-Frequency Adjectives

Base	en	ett	plural
stor (big)	stor	stort	stora
liten (small)	liten	litet	små
gammal (old)	gammal	gammalt	gamla
ny (new)	ny	nytt	nya
fin (nice)	fin	fint	fina

Swedish learners need to notice how meaning is built through:

• prepositions
• articles (en / ett)
• definite forms
• word combinations
• sentence position

In Swedish, prepositions are shown with:
• i = in / inside
• på = on / at
• från = from
• till = to
• med = with
• utan = without
• som = as

Swedish also uses:
• definite endings instead of separate words

- bok → boken (the book)
- hus → huset (the house)

If you can recognize what the preposition or form is doing, you are already understanding Swedish correctly.

Swedish Meaning Patterns

Recognition, Not Memorization

Swedish usually expresses relationships such as place, movement, possession, direction, and role through **prepositions and word forms**, not noun case endings.

You do not need to memorize everything at once.
If you can recognize the pattern and understand the meaning, you are already using Swedish well.

This chapter is about recognition — not grammar study.

Common Meaning Patterns in Swedish

Swedish Pattern	What it answers	Example	English Meaning
basic noun	who? what?	bok	book
possessive (-s)	whose?	elevens bok	the student's book
i	where? in?	i bilen	in the car
från	from where?	från bilen	from the car
till	to where?	till huset	to the house
med	with whom?	med en vän	with a friend
utan	without what?	utan kaffe	without coffee
som	as what?	som lärare	as a teacher
bli / bli	becoming	blev lugn	became calm

Swedish Patterns to Notice

Swedish often uses small connecting words and word forms instead of endings.
These patterns show place, possession, movement, and role.

Pattern (Swedish)	Pattern (English)
Detta är en/ett {substantiv}.	This is a {noun}.
{Substantiv}-s {substantiv}.	The {noun}'s {noun}.

Pattern (Swedish)	Pattern (English)
Jag är i {plats}.	I am in {place}.
Jag kom från {plats}.	I came from {place}.
Jag går till {plats}.	I go to {place}.
Jag är med {substantiv}.	I am with {noun}.
Jag gick utan {substantiv}.	I left without {noun}.
Jag arbetar som {substantiv}.	I work as a {noun}.
Jag blev {adjektiv}.	I became {adj}.

Swedish in a Dialog

Jag har en bok.	I have a book.
Jag behöver boken till imorgon.	I need the book for tomorrow.
Jag läser boken på kvällen.	I read the book in the evening.
Vi går till biblioteket tillsammans.	We are going to the library together.
Vi är i biblioteket nu.	We are now in the library.
Vi går från biblioteket snart.	We'll leave the library soon.
Jag lägger boken på bordet för dig.	I'll leave the book on the table for you.
Tack! Den är redan på bordet.	Thanks! It's already on the table.
Jag tar boken från bordet en stund.	I'll take it off the table for a moment.
Jag tittade ut genom fönstret.	I looked out of the window.
Jag gick förbi fönstret.	I walked past the window.
Jag bor i ett hus här nära.	I live in a nearby house.
Jag pratade med en vän länge.	I spoke with a friend for a long time.

Jag åker till staden imorgon.	I'm leaving for the city tomorrow.
Jag kommer från staden på lördag.	I'll come from the city on Saturday.
Sedan stannar vi i staden för kaffe.	Then we'll stop in the city for coffee.
Allt är klart för vännen.	Everything is ready for the friend.

Mini Recognition Table

with butik ("shop")

Pattern	Example	Meaning
basic form	butik	shop
definite form	butiken	the shop
i	i butiken	in the shop
till	till butiken	to the shop
från	från butiken	from the shop
med	med butiken / med någon från butiken	with / connected to the shop
utan	utan butiken	without the shop

Small Conversation About Swedish Meaning Patterns

Tiina, varför sa du i butiken men också till butiken?	Tiina, why did you say in the shop, but also to the shop?
För att vi använder prepositioner för att visa plats och riktning.	Because we use prepositions to show place and direction.
Hur menar du?	What do you mean?

"I butiken" visar var någon är.	"In the shop" shows where someone is.
Och "till butiken"?	And "to the shop"?
Det visar rörelse mot platsen.	That shows movement toward the place.
Aha, så de små orden visar relationen?	Ah, so the little words show the relationship?
Precis. På svenska gör de små orden mycket arbete.	Exactly. In Swedish, those small words do a lot of work.

Key Idea:
Swedish uses **small words and word forms** (prepositions + definite endings) to show meaning.
If you recognize these patterns, you are already understanding Swedish.

Engine 202: Verbmönster du redan använder

Om du har talat genom engines i den här boken, har du redan använt svenska verb korrekt många gånger.

Det här kapitlet börjar inte från noll.
Det hjälper dig att **känna igen de verbmönster du redan kan**.

På svenska förändras verb mycket lite.
Istället visas betydelse genom:
• tid (nu eller då)
• hjälpverb (ska, vill, kan)
• ordföljd
• små ord i meningen

Du behöver inte memorera alla regler nu.
Om du känner igen mönstret och förstår betydelsen, använder du redan riktig svenska.

Det här kapitlet handlar om igenkänning — inte om tung grammatik.

Verbmönster du redan använder

Mönster	Vad det gör	Exempel du redan har använt
Presens	vad som händer nu	jag gör, jag går, jag tänker
Preteritum	vad som redan hände	jag gjorde, jag gick, jag lärde mig
Negation	säga nej / inte	jag vet inte, det gör inget
Fråga	ställa en fråga	Pratar du svenska?
Modal betydelse	vilja, kunna, måste	jag vill, jag kan, jag måste
Konditional / artigt	hypotetiskt / artigt	jag skulle vilja, jag skulle kunna
Progressiv (kontext)	händer just nu	jag håller på att göra
Infinitiv	namnge en handling	göra, gå, lära

Du behöver inte memorera detta kapitel.
Kom tillbaka till det när nyfikenheten uppstår.
Flyt utvecklas genom igenkänning — inte förklaring.

Svenska verb och pronomen

På svenska ändras verb nästan inte beroende på person.
Pronomen används alltid för att visa vem som gör handlingen.

Du har redan sett dessa mönster i engines i den här boken.

Pronomenlista

Person	Pronomen	Verbform	Exempel
jag	jag	samma form	jag pratar, jag går
du	du	samma form	du pratar, du går
han / hon	han / hon	samma form	han pratar, hon går
vi	vi	samma form	vi pratar, vi går
ni	ni	samma form	ni pratar, ni går
de	de	samma form	de pratar, de går

Mini-konversation: Svenska verb i verklig användning

Tiina, varför säger du jag går men också jag gick?	Tiina, why do you say jag går but also jag gick?
För att verb visar tid — nu eller då.	Because verbs show time — now or then.
Så går är nu och gick är tidigare?	So går is now and gick is before?
Precis. Går är presens och gick är dåtid.	Exactly. Går is present and gick is past.
Och inte?	And what about not?
Det är negation: jag vet / jag vet inte.	That's negation: I know / I don't know.
Så jag har redan använt allt detta?	So I've already used all this?
Ja! Du använder redan mycket mer svenska än du tror.	Yes! You already use far more Swedish than you think.

Pattern Overview (Swedish)

Pattern	What it does	Example
Present tense	What is happening now	jag talar, jag går
Past tense	What already happened	jag talade, jag gick
Future meaning	What will happen	jag ska gå
Negative form	Saying no / not	jag talar inte
Question form	Asking	Talar du svenska?
Modal verbs	Want, can, must	vill, kan, måste
Conditional	Polite / hypothetical	skulle vilja
Passive voice	General / unknown subject	det görs

Pattern	What it does	Example
Infinitive	Naming an action	att tala, att gå

Core Insight (VERY IMPORTANT)

Swedish verbs **do NOT change by person**

jag talar	I speak
du talar	you speak
han talar	he speaks
vi talar	we speak

One form = all persons

Present Tense (Now)

jag går	I go
jag äter	I eat
jag tänker	I think

Usually ends in **-r**

Past Tense (Before)

jag gick	I went
jag åt	I ate
jag tänkte	I thought

Often **-de / -te** or irregular

Future (Simple Pattern)

jag ska gå	I will go

jag ska läsa I will read

ska + verb (infinitive)

Negative Form

Add **inte**

jag vet inte I don't know

jag går inte I don't go

Question Form (Word Order Shift)

Verb comes first

Talar du svenska? Do you speak Swedish?

Kommer du idag? Are you coming today?

Modal Verbs (VERY COMMON)

jag vill I want

jag kan I can

jag måste I must

Pattern:

modal + verb (infinitive)

jag vill gå I want to go

jag kan läsa I can read

Conditional (Polite / Soft)

jag skulle vilja I would like

jag skulle kunna I could

Passive Voice

det görs it is done

det sägs it is said

Often ends in **-s**

Infinitive (To Do)

Usually uses **att**

att gå to go

att äta to eat

Mini Dialog (Real Usage)

Talar du svenska?	Do you speak Swedish?
Ja, jag lär mig fortfarande.	Yes, I am still learning.
Vill du öva tillsammans?	Do you want to practice together?
Ja, jag vill gärna göra det.	Yes, I would like that.
Vi kan börja nu.	We can start now.
Bra, jag är redo.	Good, I am ready.
Förstår du allt?	Do you understand everything?
Inte allt, men jag lär mig.	Not everything, but I'm learning.
Det är så man blir bättre.	That's how you improve.
Ja, vi fortsätter.	Yes, let's continue.

Kärnidé:
Svenska verb är enkla mönster.
Om du känner igen dem, använder du redan språket.

Engine 203: Vardagsnyheter & gemensam verklighet

Detta kapitel samlar vanliga svenska ord och uttryck som används för att tala om vardagliga händelser, gemensam verklighet och situationer som utvecklas.

Målet är inte debatt.
Målet är igenkänning, lugn diskussion och praktiskt språk.

Du kan höra dessa uttryck i samtal, i nyheter, online eller i vardagen.

Ordförråd för gemensam verklighet (lätt och neutralt användning)

Kategori	Svenska	English	How it's typically used
Grundverb	hända / ske	to happen	neutral description of events
	berätta / rapportera	to tell / report	summarizing information
	påverka / beröra	to affect	"this affects…"
	ha att göra med / relatera till	to relate to	connecting topics
	fortsätta	to continue	ongoing situations
	förändras / ändras	to change	non-judgmental change
	verka	to seem	softening statements
	bli klart / klargöras	to become clear	uncertainty-friendly
Vanliga substantiv	nyhet	news item	individual piece of news
	situation	situation	current state of things
	förändring	change	factual shift
	beslut	decision	official or informal

Kategori	Svenska	English	How it's typically used
	studie	study	research, reports
	information	information	known facts
	fråga / ärende	issue	general topic
	ämne	topic	what's being discussed

Neutrala fraser (trygga öppningar)

Svenska	English	How it's typically used
Har du hört om det här?	Have you heard about this?	neutral opener
Man vet inte allt än.	Not everything is known yet.	signals restraint
Vi får se hur situationen utvecklas.	Let's see how it develops.	calm close
Det påverkar många människor.	This affects many people.	factual framing
Det är svårt att säga än.	Hard to say yet.	neutral restraint

Tonmarkörer (lugnt och neutralt)

Svenska	English	How it's typically used
inget dramatiskt	nothing dramatic	downplays intensity
ganska lugnt	fairly calmly	neutral tone
försiktigt sagt	cautiously speaking	hedging claims

Mini dialog: Vardagsnyheter och gemensam verklighet

Svenska	English
Har du hört om det här?	Have you heard about this?
Lite, men jag förstår inte allt ännu.	I heard a little, but I still don't understand everything.
Ja, man vet inte allt än.	Yes, not everything is known yet.
Påverkar det många människor?	Does this affect many people?
Det verkar så, men det är svårt att säga säkert.	It seems so, but it's still hard to say for sure.
Då är det bättre att följa det lugnt.	Then it's better to follow it calmly.
Ja, vi får se hur situationen utvecklas.	Yes, let's see how the situation develops.

Kärnidé:
Att tala om verkligheten betyder inte att debattera.
Lugnt och neutralt språk är ett tecken på avancerad språklig förmåga.

Engine 204: Travel & Mobility

Hej, jag har en bokning i namnet Anderson.	Hi, I have a reservation under the name Anderson.
Välkommen. Får jag se ditt pass?	Welcome. May I see your passport?
Här, varsågod.	Here you are.
Vill du ha frukost inkluderad?	Would you like breakfast included?
Ja, tack.	Yes, please.
Ditt rum är på tredje våningen.	Your room is on the third floor.
Vilken tid är utcheckning?	What time is check-out?

Utcheckning är klockan 12.	Check-out is at 12.
Tack så mycket.	Thank you very much.
Ha en trevlig vistelse!	Enjoy your stay!

Engine 205: Doctor Visit Regarding Health & Symptoms

Jag behöver boka en läkartid.	I need to book a doctor's appointment.
Vad är problemet?	What seems to be the problem?
Jag har haft feber och hosta i tre dagar.	I've had a fever and a cough for three days.
Har du ont i bröstet eller halsen?	Do you have pain in your chest or throat?
Halsen är verkligen öm och jag känner mig trött.	My throat is very sore and I feel tired.
Vi tar ett blodprov och ett halsprov för säkerhets skull.	We'll take a blood test and a throat swab just in case.
Hur länge tar återhämtningen?	How long will recovery take?
Förmodligen ungefär en vecka. Vila och drick mycket vatten.	Probably about a week. Rest and drink plenty of water.
Tack för hjälpen.	Thank you for your help.
Krya på dig!	Get well soon!

Engine 206: Talking to Police for Safety & Directions

Ursäkta, jag behöver hjälp.	Excuse me, I need help.
Vad har hänt?	What happened?

Jag tappade min plånbok på bussen.	I lost my wallet on the bus.
När hände det här?	When did this happen?
För ungefär en timme sedan i centrum.	About an hour ago downtown.
Har du någon legitimation?	Do you have any identification?
Ja, jag har mitt pass med mig.	Yes, I have my passport with me.
Vi gör en anmälan och hjälper dig.	We'll make a report and help you.
Tack så mycket.	Thank you very much.
Ingen orsak.	You're welcome.

Engine 207: Ordering Coffee & Café Life

Hej, kan jag få en kaffe?	Hi, could I get a coffee?
Självklart! Vilken sorts kaffe vill du ha?	Of course! What kind of coffee would you like?
En latte med havremjölk, tack.	A latte with oat milk, please.
Vill du ha något att äta?	Would you like something to eat?
Ja, en chokladcroissant.	Yes, a chocolate croissant.
Att ta med eller äta här?	To go or for here?
Att ta med, tack.	To go, please.
Det blir 6 euro.	That will be 6 euros.
Tack!	Thank you!
Varsågod, ha en bra dag!	You're welcome, have a nice day!

Engine 208: Ordering Breakfast, Lunch or Dinner

Hej, kan vi få menyn?	Hi, can we get the menu?
Självklart, varsågod.	Of course, here you go.
Jag är redo att beställa.	I'm ready to order.
Vad rekommenderar du?	What do you recommend?
Dagens pasta är populär.	The pasta of the day is popular.
Jag tar den och ett glas vatten.	I'll take that and a glass of water.
Vill ni ha efterrätt senare?	Would you like dessert later?
Vi får se senare, tack.	We'll see later, thanks.
Tack, maten kommer snart.	Thank you, your food will be ready soon.

Engine 209: Ordering on the Phone - Pizza / Delivery

Hej, jag vill göra en beställning.	Hello, I'd like to place an order.
Vad vill du beställa?	What would you like to order?
En stor vegetarisk pizza och en cola.	A large veggie pizza and a cola.
Vad är din adress?	What is your address?
Gata 10, lägenhet 5.	Street 10, apartment 5.
Hur lång tid tar leveransen?	How long will delivery take?
Cirka 30 minuter.	About 30 minutes.
Hur kan jag betala?	How can I pay?
Med kort vid dörren.	By card at the door.
Tack för din beställning!	Thank you for your order!

Engine 210: Asking for Directions

Ursäkta, var ligger tågstationen?	Excuse me, where is the train station?
Den ligger ungefär fem minuters promenad bort.	It's about a five-minute walk away.
Behöver jag svänga vänster?	Do I need to turn left?
Ja, sväng vänster och fortsätt rakt fram.	Yes, turn left and continue straight.
Ligger den nära banken?	Is it near the bank?
Ja, den ligger bredvid banken.	Yes, it's next to the bank.
Tack för hjälpen!	Thank you for the help!
Ingen orsak.	You're welcome.

Engine 211: Airport & Flying

Var är incheckningen?	Where is check-in?
Den är där borta till höger.	It's over there on the right.
Här är mitt boardingkort.	Here is my boarding pass.
Har du bagage att checka in?	Do you have luggage to check in?
Ja, en resväska.	Yes, one suitcase.
Gate har ändrats.	The gate has changed.
Vad är den nya gaten?	What is the new gate?
Gate 24.	Gate 24.
Tack för informationen.	Thank you for the information.

Engine 212: Shopping & Services in a Store

Kan jag hjälpa dig?	Can I help you?
Jag letar efter den här skjortan i en större storlek.	I'm looking for this shirt in a larger size.
Vilken storlek har du?	What size are you?
Storlek M.	Size M.
Vill du prova den?	Would you like to try it on?
Ja, var är provrummet?	Yes, where is the fitting room?
Det är där bak.	It's in the back.
Jag tar den här.	I'll take this.
Kan jag betala med kort?	Can I pay by card?
Självklart.	Of course.

Engine 213: Grocery Store & Services

Var är mjölken?	Where is the milk?
Den är på tredje hyllan.	It's on the third shelf.
Behöver de här vägas?	Do these need to be weighed?
Ja, vågen är där borta.	Yes, the scale is over there.
Hittade du allt?	Did you find everything?
Ja, tack.	Yes, thank you.
Vill du ha kvitto?	Would you like a receipt?
Ja, tack.	Yes, please.

Engine 214: Meeting New People, Social Life & Relationships

Hej, jag heter Mark.	Hi, I'm Mark.
Trevligt att träffas, jag är Anna.	Nice to meet you, I'm Anna.
Var kommer du ifrån?	Where are you from?
Jag kommer från USA.	I'm from the United States.
Hur länge har du bott här?	How long have you lived here?
Ungefär två år.	About two years.
Vad jobbar du med?	What do you do for work?
Jag är forskare.	I'm a researcher.
Det var trevligt att träffas.	It was nice meeting you.

Engine 215: Bank / Payment Issue

Mitt kort fungerar inte.	My card isn't working.
Vill du försöka igen?	Would you like to try again?
Ja, tack.	Yes, please.
Det verkar som att betalningen inte godkändes.	It seems the payment was declined.
Kan jag betala kontant?	Can I pay in cash?
Självklart.	Of course.
Jag behöver också ett kontoutdrag.	I also need a bank statement.
Vi kan skriva ut det åt dig.	We can print it for you.

Engine 216: Emergency Call or Critical Situation

Jag behöver en ambulans omedelbart.	I need an ambulance immediately.

Vad är din nödsituation? What is your emergency?

Min vän andas inte ordentligt. My friend isn't breathing properly.

Var är ni? Where are you?

Adressen är Gata 5. The address is Street 5.

Hjälp är på väg. Help is on the way.

Tack. Thank you.

Stanna kvar i linjen. Stay on the line.

Engine 217: Pharmacy, Health & Medicine

Hej, jag behöver medicin mot förkylning. Hi, I need medicine for a cold.

Vilka symptom har du? What symptoms do you have?

Jag har ont i halsen och feber. I have a sore throat and a fever.

Jag rekommenderar det här läkemedlet. I recommend this medicine.

Hur ofta ska jag ta det? How often should I take it?

Två gånger om dagen. Twice a day.

Behöver jag recept? Do I need a prescription?

Nej, det här är receptfritt. No, this is over the counter.

Tack för hjälpen. Thank you for the help.

Engine 218: Making Social Life Plans

Vill du träffas imorgon? Would you like to meet tomorrow?

Låter bra. Sounds good.

Ska vi gå och ta en kaffe? Shall we go for coffee?

Vilken tid passar?	What time works?
Klockan tre passar mig.	Three o'clock works for me.
Var ska vi träffas?	Where shall we meet?
Vi träffas på ett café i centrum.	Let's meet at the café downtown.
Vi ses imorgon!	See you tomorrow!

Engine 219: Buying Public Transportation, Tickets, Travel

Jag vill köpa en bussbiljett.	I'd like to buy a bus ticket.
Vart reser du?	Where are you traveling to?
Till centrum, tack.	To downtown, please.
Enkel eller tur och retur?	One way or return?
Tur och retur.	Return.
Det blir 5 euro.	That will be 5 euros.
Kan jag betala med kort?	Can I pay by card?
Ja. Här är din biljett.	Yes. Here is your ticket.

Engine 220: Housing / Landlord

Hej, jag har ett problem i lägenheten.	Hi, I have a problem in the apartment.
Vad är fel?	What's wrong?
Värmen fungerar inte.	The heating isn't working.
Vi kommer att fixa det imorgon.	We will fix it tomorrow.
Tack så mycket.	Thank you very much.
Är det något annat?	Is there anything else?

Nej, det är allt.	No, that's all.

Engine 221: Post Office / Package Pickup

Hej, jag fick en avisering om ett paket.	Hi, I received a notice about a package.
Får jag se din legitimation?	May I see your ID?
Här.	Here it is.
Här är ditt paket.	Here is your package.
Tack så mycket.	Thank you very much.

Engine 222: Restaurant Problem

Ursäkta, maten är kall.	Excuse me, the food is cold.
Jag är ledsen för det.	I'm sorry about that.
Kan vi få en ny portion?	Could we get a new portion?
Självklart, genast.	Of course, right away.
Tack så mycket.	Thank you very much.

Engine 223: Taxi Ride

Jag behöver en taxi.	I need a taxi.
Vart vill du åka?	Where would you like to go?
Till flygplatsen, tack.	To the airport, please.
Hur lång tid tar resan?	How long will the trip take?
Ungefär 20 minuter.	About 20 minutes.

Tack för resan.	Thank you for the ride.

Engine 224: Hairdresser or Barber

Jag skulle vilja klippa håret.	I'd like a haircut.
Hur mycket vill du klippa?	How much would you like cut?
Bara lite kortare.	Just a little shorter.
Vill du ha tvätt?	Would you like a wash?
Ja, tack.	Yes, please.
Klart!	All done!

Engine 225: Visiting Someone's Home

Tack för inbjudan.	Thank you for the invitation.
Välkommen!	Welcome!
Det här hemmet är vackert.	This home is beautiful.
Vill du ha något att dricka?	Would you like something to drink?
Ja tack, gärna.	Yes please, thank you.
Det var trevligt att hälsa på.	It was nice visiting.

Engine 226: Small Talk at Work

God morgon!	Good morning!
Hur var din helg?	How was your weekend?
Den var avkopplande.	It was relaxing.

Vad gjorde du?	What did you do?
Jag gick en promenad och läste en bok.	I went for a walk and read a book.

Engine 227: Phone or Internet Service

Jag behöver ett nytt SIM-kort.	I need a new SIM card.
Vill du ha ett datapaket?	Would you like a data plan?
Ja, obegränsad data.	Yes, unlimited data.
När fungerar det?	When will it work?
Direkt.	Immediately.

Engine 228: Job Interview

Tack för att du kom till intervjun.	Thank you for coming to the interview.
Tack för inbjudan.	Thank you for the invitation.
Kan du berätta om dig själv?	Can you tell us about yourself?
Jag har fem års erfarenhet inom området.	I have five years of experience in the field.
Varför vill du ha det här jobbet?	Why do you want this job?
Jag är intresserad av ert företag och rollen.	I'm interested in your company and the role.
När kan du börja?	When can you start?
Jag kan börja nästa månad.	I can start next month.
Tack för din tid.	Thank you for your time.

Engine 229: First Day at Work

Hej, jag är den nya medarbetaren.	Hi, I'm the new employee.
Välkommen till teamet!	Welcome to the team!
Kan du visa mig kontoret?	Could you show me the office?
Självklart.	Of course.
Var är fikarummet?	Where is the break room?
Det är i slutet av korridoren.	It's at the end of the hallway.
Tack för hjälpen.	Thank you for the help.

Engine 230: School, University or Education

När börjar lektionen?	Where does the class begin?
Den börjar klockan nio.	It starts at nine o'clock.
Behöver vi en lärobok?	Do we need a textbook?
Ja, den här boken.	Yes, this book.
När är tentamen?	When is the exam?
Nästa månad.	Next month.
Tack för informationen.	Thank you for the information.

Engine 231: Gym and Fitness

Jag skulle vilja ha ett gymmedlemskap.	I'd like a gym membership.
Per månad eller per år?	Monthly or yearly?
Per månad, tack.	Monthly, please.

Behöver du en introduktion? Do you need an introduction?

Ja, gärna. Yes, please.

Välkommen att träna! Welcome to work out!

Engine 232: Hobby Course

Jag skulle vilja gå med i en kurs. I'd like to join the course.

Vilken kurs är du intresserad av? Which course interests you?

Fotokursen. The photography course.

Den börjar nästa vecka. It starts next week.

Perfekt, jag anmäler mig. Great, I'll sign up.

Engine 233: Customer Service and Complaint

Jag skulle vilja göra en reklamation. I'd like to make a complaint.

Vad är problemet? What is the problem?

Produkten är trasig. The product is broken.

Vill du ha återbetalning eller byte? Would you like a refund or exchange?

Återbetalning, tack. A refund, please.

Vi tar hand om det direkt. We'll handle it right away.

Engine 234: Childcare School Parent Talk

Hur var mitt barns dag? How was my child's day?

Hen hade en bra dag. They had a good day.

Åt hen bra?	Did they eat well?
Ja, allt gick bra.	Yes, everything went well.
Tack så mycket.	Thank you very much.

Engine 235: Making a Phone Appointment

Jag skulle vilja boka en tid.	I'd like to book an appointment.
För vilken dag?	For which day?
Till nästa måndag.	For next Monday.
Vilken tid passar?	What time works?
Klockan tio.	Ten o'clock.
Tiden är bokad.	The appointment is booked.

Engine 236: Talking About the Weather

Det är verkligen kallt idag.	It's really cold today.
Ja, vintern kom tidigt.	Yes, winter arrived early.
Kommer det att regna imorgon?	Will it rain tomorrow?
Enligt prognosen, ja.	According to the forecast, yes.
Förhoppningsvis skiner solen i helgen.	Hopefully the sun will shine this weekend.
Vi får hoppas det.	Let's hope so.

Engine 237: Holidays & Celebrations

Vad gör du till jul?	What are you doing for Christmas?
Jag tillbringar tid med familjen.	I'm spending time with family.
Och på nyår?	What about New Year's?
Jag går på en fest med vänner.	I'm going to a party with friends.
Låter trevligt!	Sounds nice!

Engine 238: Invitations & Events

Vill du komma på fest på lördag?	Would you like to come to a party on Saturday?
Låter kul!	Sounds fun!
När börjar festen?	What time do the party start?
Klockan sju.	At seven o'clock.
Vi ses där!	See you there!

Engine 239: Technology Help

Internet fungerar inte.	The internet isn't working.
Har ni startat om routern?	Have you restarted the router?
Ja, men problemet kvarstår.	Yes, but the problem continues.
Vi skickar en tekniker imorgon.	We'll send a technician tomorrow.
Tack för hjälpen.	Thank you for the help.

Engine 240: Saying Goodbye and Moving Away

Jag flyttar nästa månad.	I'm moving next month.
Åh nej, vart ska du?	Oh no, where are you going?
Till en annan stad för arbete.	To another city for work.
Låt oss hålla kontakten.	Let's stay in touch.
Självklart.	Of course.
Det var ett nöje att träffas.	It was a pleasure meeting you.

Engine 241: Gas Station and Fuel

Hej, var kan jag tanka?	Hi, where can I refuel?
Pumparna är där ute.	The pumps are outside.
Betalar jag först eller efteråt?	Do I pay first or after?
Du kan betala inne efteråt.	You can pay inside afterwards.
Jag fyllde tanken.	I filled the tank.
Det blir 65 euro.	That will be 65 euros.
Kan jag betala med kort?	Can I pay by card?
Självklart.	Of course.
Tack, trevlig resa!	Thank you, have a good trip!

Engine 242: Car Repair and Mechanic

Min bil låter konstigt.	My car is making a strange noise.
När började problemet?	When did the problem start?
Igår kväll.	Yesterday evening.
Lämna bilen här för kontroll.	Please leave the car here for inspection.

Hur länge tar reparationen?	How long will the repair take?
Förmodligen två dagar.	Probably two days.
Tack för hjälpen.	Thank you for the help.

Engine 243: Government Office Registration

Hej, jag behöver registrera min adress.	Hi, I need to register my address.
Fyll i det här formuläret.	Please fill in this form.
Behöver ni passet?	Do you need a passport?
Ja, och ett adressbevis.	Yes, and proof of address.
Här är dokumenten.	Here are the documents.
Registreringen är klar.	The registration is complete.
Tack så mycket.	Thank you very much.

Engine 244: Hospital Visiting Someone

Jag är här för att besöka min vän.	I'm here to visit my friend.
Vad är patientens namn?	What is the patient's name?
Anna Virtanen.	Anna Virtanen.
Hon är i rum 203.	She is in room 203.
Kan jag ta med blommor?	Can I bring flowers?
Ja, men ingen mat.	Yes, but no food.
Tack för informationen.	Thank you for the information.

Engine 245: Online Order and Returning a Package

Jag vill returnera den här produkten.	I'd like to return this product.
Vad är ordernumret?	What is the order number?
Här är kvittot.	Here is the receipt.
Vad är orsaken till returen?	What is the reason for the return?
Produkten passade mig inte.	The product didn't suit me.
Returen är godkänd.	The return is approved.
Pengarna återbetalas inom fem dagar.	The money will be refunded in five days.

Engine 246: Time, Dates & Numbers Overview

måndag • tisdag • onsdag • torsdag • fredag • lördag • söndag	Mon • Tue • Wed • Thu • Fri • Sat • Sun
på måndag = on Monday • på söndag = on Sunday	on Monday • on Sunday
Idag är det måndag.	Today is Monday.
Imorgon är det tisdag.	Tomorrow is Tuesday.
Igår var det söndag.	Yesterday was Sunday.
Vi ses på fredag.	See you on Friday.

Swedish	English
januari Jan • februari Feb • mars Mar • april Apr • maj May • juni Jun	Jan • Feb • Mar • Apr • May • Jun
juli Jul • augusti Aug • september Sep • oktober Oct • november Nov • december Dec	Jul • Aug • Sep • Oct • Nov • Dec

Swedish	English
i januari = in January • i juli = in July	in January • in July
Det är januari nu.	It is January.
Nästa månad är det februari.	Next month is February.
Förra månaden var det december.	Last month was December.
Vi reser i juli.	We travel in July.
Kursen börjar i september.	The course starts in September.

Swedish	English
5 maj	May 5
10 juli	July 10
1 januari	January 1
Vilket datum är det idag?	What's the date today?

Swedish	English
noll 0 • ett 1 • två 2 • tre 3 • fyra 4 • fem 5 • sex 6 • sju 7 • åtta 8 • nio 9 • tio 10	0 • 1 • 2 • 3 • 4 • 5 • 6 • 7 • 8 • 9 • 10
elva 11 • tolv 12 • tretton 13 • fjorton 14 • femton 15	11 • 12 • 13 • 14 • 15
sexton 16 • sjutton 17 • arton 18 • nitton 19	16 • 17 • 18 • 19
tjugo 20 • trettio 30 • fyrtio 40 • femtio 50	20 • 30 • 40 • 50
sextio 60 • sjuttio 70 • åttio 80 • nittio 90	60 • 70 • 80 • 90
hundra 100 • tusen 1000	100 • 1000

Swedish	English
Jag är 30 år gammal.	I am 30 years old.
Hur gammal är du?	How old are you?

Swedish	English
Mitt telefonnummer är…	My phone number is…
Kan du upprepa?	Could you repeat that?

Vad är klockan?	What time is it?
klockan tre	3:00
halv fyra	3:30
halv sex	5:30
kvart över tre	3:15
kvart i fyra	3:45
klockan 3.10 • klockan 7.25 • klockan 9.40	3.10 • 7.25 • 9.40
klockan sju	at seven

Engine 247: How Was Your Evening?

Hur var din kväll igår?	How was your evening yesterday?
Ganska bra, jag var bara hemma och tittade lite på TV.	Pretty good, I just stayed home and watched some TV.
Åh, avslappnat! Vad tittade du på?	Oh, relaxing! What did you watch?
En dokumentär. Den var förvånansvärt bra.	A documentary. It was surprisingly good.

Trevligt, vad var den bästa delen?	Nice, what was the best part?
Den fick mig att tänka på saker på ett nytt sätt.	It made me think about things differently.
Vad bra, tack för att du berättade.	That's great, thanks for sharing.
Vi fortsätter senare!	Let's continue later!

Engine 248: I Broke My Leg Skiing

Jag är ledsen, jag råkade ut för en olycka.	I'm sorry, I had an accident.
Åh nej, vad hände?	Oh no, what happened?
Jag bröt benet när jag åkte skidor.	I broke my leg while skiing.
Oj, det låter allvarligt. Var hände det?	Oh wow, that sounds serious. Where did it happen?
I backen, jag föll i hög fart.	On the slope, I fell at high speed.
Gjorde det ont direkt?	Did it hurt immediately?
Ja, jag kunde inte resa mig.	Yes, I couldn't stand up.
Ringde du efter hjälp?	Did you call for help?
Ja, jag fördes till sjukhuset med ambulans.	Yes, I was taken to the hospital by ambulance.
Vad sa läkaren?	What did the doctor say?
Benet är brutet, men det kommer att läka med tiden.	The leg is fractured, but it will heal with time.
Hur länge tar återhämtningen?	How long will recovery take?
Cirka sex veckor i gips.	About six weeks in a cast.
Har du ont nu?	Are you in pain now?
Lite, men medicinen hjälper.	A little, but the medication helps.

Behöver du hjälp hemma?	Do you need help at home?
Kanske i början, det är svårt att röra sig.	Maybe at first, moving around is difficult.
Jag önskar dig en snabb återhämtning.	I wish you a speedy recovery.
Tack så mycket, jag uppskattar det.	Thank you very much, I appreciate that.

Engine 249: Reporting an Incident to Police

Hej, jag vill anmäla en sak.	Hello, I would like to report something.
Självklart. Vad gäller det?	Of course. What is it about?
Min cykel blev stulen igår kväll.	My bicycle was stolen last night.
Var och när hände det?	Where and at what time did this happen?
Det var nära tågstationen runt klockan åtta.	It was near the train station around eight o'clock.
Var cykeln låst?	Was the bicycle locked?
Ja, den var fastlåst vid ett ställ.	Yes, it was attached to a rack.
Har du en bild eller ramnummer?	Do you have a photo or the frame number?
Ja, jag har båda i min telefon.	Yes, I have both on my phone.
Bra. Vi gör en anmälan.	Good. We will file a report.
Vad händer härnäst?	What happens next?
Du får ett ärendenummer, och vi kontaktar dig om vi får mer information.	You will receive a report number, and we will contact you if we get more information.
Behöver jag göra något mer?	Do I need to do anything else?

Inte just nu, men spara all relaterad information.	Not at the moment, but keep all related information.
Tack för hjälpen.	Thank you for your assistance.
Varsågod. Vi hoppas att det löser sig snart.	You're welcome. Hopefully the matter will be resolved soon.

Engine 250: Being Questioned as a Witness

Jag förstår att ni vill fråga mig om det som hände.	I understand you would like to ask me about what happened.
Ja. Var befann du dig vid tidpunkten?	Yes. Where were you at the time?
Jag var på andra sidan gatan, cirka tio meter bort.	I was across the street, about ten meters away.
Såg du själv situationen?	Did you personally see the situation?
Jag såg en del av det, men inte allt.	I saw part of it, but not everything.
Kan du beskriva vad du såg?	Can you describe what you saw?
Jag såg två personer prata högljutt innan en av dem gick därifrån snabbt.	I saw two people arguing loudly before one of them left quickly.
Hörde du något specifikt?	Did you hear anything specific?
Inte tydligt, bara höjda röster.	Not clearly, only raised voices.
Tack för ditt samarbete.	Thank you for your cooperation.
Självklart. Jag vill hjälpa så gott jag kan.	Of course. I want to help as best I can.

Engine 251: Traffic Stop Explanation

God kväll. Vet du varför vi stoppade dig?	Good evening. Do you know why we stopped you?
Jag är inte säker. Kan du förklara?	I'm not sure. Could you clarify?
Du körde något över hastighetsgränsen.	You were driving slightly over the speed limit.
Jag förstår. Jag märkte inte att hastighetsgränsen ändrades.	I understand. I didn't notice the speed limit had changed.
Har du körkort och registreringsbevis med dig?	Do you have your license and registration?
Ja, här är de.	Yes, here they are.
Detta är en varning. Var mer uppmärksam i fortsättningen.	This is a warning. Please be more careful in the future.
Tack för informationen. Jag uppskattar förklaringen.	Thank you for the information. I appreciate the clarification.

Engine 252: Filing a Formal Written Statement

Jag blev ombedd att lämna ett skriftligt uttalande.	I was asked to provide a written statement.
Ja. Du kan börja med att beskriva händelserna i kronologisk ordning.	Yes. You may begin by describing the events in chronological order.
Händelsen började ungefär klockan 18.30.	The incident began at approximately 6:30 p.m.
Var det andra personer närvarande?	Were there other individuals present?
Ja, minst tre andra personer.	Yes, at least three other individuals.
Är din redogörelse fullständig och sanningsenlig?	Is your account complete and truthful?
Ja, såvitt jag vet.	Yes, to the best of my knowledge.

Tack. Uttalandet kommer att bifogas utredningen.	Thank you. The statement will be attached to the investigation.

Engine 253: Explaining an Accident with Another Driver

Tyvärr krockade vi i korsningen.	Unfortunately, we collided at the intersection.
Blev någon skadad?	Was anyone injured?
Inte allvarligt, men båda bilarna skadades.	Not seriously, but both cars were damaged.
Hur utvecklade sig situationen?	How did the situation unfold?
Jag körde rakt fram när den andra bilen svängde framför mig.	I was driving straight when the other car turned in front of me.
Har du försäkringsuppgifter med dig?	Do you have your insurance information?
Ja, vi kan utbyta uppgifter nu.	Yes, we can exchange details now.
Låt oss också göra en skadeanmälan.	Let's also file a damage report.

Engine 254: Asking About Legal Rights Politely

Jag vill försäkra mig om mina rättigheter i den här situationen.	I would like to clarify my rights in this situation.
Självklart. I vilket avseende?	Of course. Regarding what?
Har jag rätt att få juridisk rådgivning?	Do I have the right to receive legal advice?
Ja, du har rätt till en advokat.	Yes, you have the right to a lawyer.
Får jag prata med en advokat innan jag svarar på frågor?	May I speak with a lawyer before answering questions?

Ja, det är möjligt.	Yes, that is possible.
Tack för förtydligandet.	Thank you for the clarification.
Varsågod.	You're welcome.

Engine 255: Choosing a Major or Field of Study

Vad studerar du på universitetet?	What field are you studying at university?
Jag studerar ekonomi, men mitt biämne är psykologi.	I study economics, but my minor is psychology.
Vad fick dig att välja det området?	What made you choose that field?
Jag ville förstå hur människor fattar beslut.	I wanted to understand how people make decisions.
Har studierna motsvarat dina förväntningar?	Has your study matched your expectations?
Delvis. Det är mer utmanande än jag trodde.	Partly. It's more challenging than I expected.
Vilken kurs har varit mest intressant för dig?	Which course has been the most interesting for you?
Beteendeekonomi. Den kopplar samman båda områdena.	Behavioral economics. It connects both fields.
Planerar du att fortsätta till en masterexamen?	Do you plan to continue to a master's degree?
Ja, men jag överväger också att studera utomlands.	Yes, but I'm also considering studying abroad.

Engine 256: Discussing a Challenging Class

Vilken kurs har varit svårast för dig hittills?	What has been your most difficult course so far?
Sannolikhetsteori. Den kräver noggrant tänkande.	Probability theory. It requires precise thinking.
Vad känns utmanande med den?	What feels challenging about it?
Även ett litet fel förändrar hela resultatet.	Even a small mistake changes the whole result.
Hur har du försökt hantera det?	How have you tried to manage it?
Jag har bildat en studiegrupp och övar regelbundet.	I formed a study group and practice regularly.
Har det hjälpt?	Has it helped?
Ja, jag förstår saker djupare nu.	Yes, I understand things more deeply now.
Tror du att svåra kurser utvecklar dig mest?	Do you think difficult courses develop you the most?
Absolut. De tvingar dig att tänka annorlunda.	Absolutely. They force you to think differently.

Engine 257: Debating an Academic Idea

Vad tycker du om påståendet att teknik försämrar koncentrationsförmågan?	What do you think about the claim that technology weakens attention spans?
Det beror på hur den används, inte bara på tekniken i sig.	It depends on how it's used, not just the technology itself.
Kan du utveckla det?	Could you elaborate?
Om tekniken används medvetet kan den till och med förbättra lärandet.	If used intentionally, it can even enhance learning.

Men vad sägs om ständiga avbrott och notiser?	But what about constant interruptions and notifications?
Det är en fråga om självdisciplin, inte verktyget.	That's a matter of discipline, not the tool.
Så ansvaret ligger hos användaren?	So the responsibility lies with the user?
Till stor del, ja.	Largely, yes.
Intressant perspektiv.	Interesting perspective.
Den här diskussionen skulle kunna fortsätta länge.	This discussion could continue for a long time.

Engine 258: Applying for a Research Position

Jag vill ansöka om tjänsten som forskningsassistent.	I would like to apply for the research assistant position.
Bra. Vad fick dig att bli intresserad av det här projektet?	Great. What made you interested in this project?
Ämnet är direkt kopplat till min avhandling.	The topic is directly related to my thesis.
Vilken erfarenhet har du av forskningsarbete?	What kind of experience do you have in research work?
Jag har deltagit i två forskningsprojekt och analyserat data.	I have participated in two research projects and analyzed data.
Hur arbetar du under press?	How do you work under pressure?
Jag delar upp uppgifter i delar och håller tidsplanen.	I break tasks into parts and stick to the schedule.
Vad hoppas du lära dig i den här rollen?	What do you hope to learn in this role?

Jag vill fördjupa mina metodologiska färdigheter. — I would like to deepen my methodological skills.

Jag vill fördjupa mina metodologiska färdigheter.	I would like to deepen my methodological skills.
Tack för din ansökan, vi återkommer snart.	Thank you for your application, we will get back to you soon.

Engine 259: Presenting a Thesis Topic

Min avhandling handlar om beslutsfattande under osäkerhet.	My thesis examines decision-making under uncertainty.
Vad fick dig att välja det här ämnet?	What made you choose this topic?
Jag är intresserad av hur människor bedömer risker.	I'm interested in how people evaluate risks.
Vilken metod tänker du använda?	What method will you use to study this?
Jag planerar att kombinera en enkätstudie och ett experimentellt upplägg.	I plan to combine a survey and an experimental design.
Vad är den centrala frågan i din forskning?	What is the central question of your research?
Hur påverkar osäkerhet rationella val?	How does uncertainty influence rational choices?
Det låter lovande.	That sounds promising.
Tack, jag ser fram emot feedback.	Thank you, I look forward to feedback.

Engine 260: Challenging a Professor Respectfully

Får jag ställa en förtydligande fråga om föreläsningen?	May I ask a clarifying question about the lecture?

Självklart.	Of course.
Du nämnde att teorin inte fungerar i praktiken i alla situationer.	You mentioned that the theory does not work in practice in all situations.
Ja.	Yes.
Kan det ändå finnas undantag där den fungerar bättre än förväntat?	Could there be exceptions where it works better than expected?
Det är en bra poäng. Vad menar du mer specifikt?	That's a good point. What do you mean specifically?
Till exempel i små grupper där det finns färre variabler.	For example, in small groups where there are fewer variables.
Intressant perspektiv.	Interesting perspective.
Tack, jag ville bara utforska idén mer brett.	Thank you, I just wanted to explore the idea more broadly.

Engine 261: Defending an Argument in a Seminar

Huvudpåståendet i min presentation är att motivation uppstår ur mening.	The main claim of my presentation is that motivation arises from meaning.
Kan du motivera det tydligare?	Could you justify that more clearly?
Studier visar att inre mening ökar engagemanget.	Studies show that internal meaning increases engagement.
Hur är det med yttre belöningar?	What about external rewards?
De kan fungera på kort sikt, men inte på lång sikt.	They may work short-term, but not long-term.
Har du ett exempel på detta?	Do you have an example of this?
Ja, flera utbildningsstudier stödjer denna iakttagelse.	Yes, several educational studies support this finding.
Tack för förtydligandet.	Thank you for the clarification.

Tack för den bra frågan.	Thank you for the good question.

Engine 262: Discussing AI and Ethics

Vad tycker du om de etiska utmaningarna med AI?	What do you think about the ethical challenges of AI?
De är mer komplexa än man ofta tror.	They are more complex than often assumed.
Vilken utmaning oroar dig mest?	Which challenge concerns you the most?
Fördelningen av ansvar mellan människor och system.	The distribution of responsibility between humans and systems.
Bör beslutsfattandet alltid stanna hos människor?	Should decision-making always remain with humans?
Åtminstone i kritiska situationer, ja.	At least in critical situations, yes.
Kan AI öka rättvisan?	Can AI increase fairness?
Det beror på data och tillsyn.	It depends on the data and oversight.
Den här diskussionen kommer säkert att fortsätta i många år.	This discussion will surely continue for years.
Och vi måste delta aktivt i den.	And we must actively participate in it.

Engine 263: Negotiating Respectfully

Jag uppskattar ert förslag, men jag skulle vilja diskutera tidsplanen.	I appreciate your proposal, but I would like to discuss the timeline.
Självklart. Vad är det som oroar dig?	Of course. What concerns you?
Jag tror att vi behöver ytterligare en vecka för att säkerställa kvaliteten.	I believe we would need one more week to ensure quality.

Är förseningen nödvändig?	Is the delay necessary?
Enligt min mening ja, om vi vill ha ett hållbart resultat.	In my view, yes, if we want a sustainable result.
Kan vi hitta en kompromiss?	Can we find a compromise?
Kanske kan vi leverera den första delen i tid och resten senare.	Perhaps we can deliver the first part on time and the rest later.
Det låter rimligt.	That sounds reasonable.
Tack för flexibiliteten.	Thank you for your flexibility.

Engine 264: Giving Constructive Feedback

Jag skulle vilja ge dig feedback på projektet.	I'd like to give you feedback on the project.
Självklart, jag lyssnar gärna.	Of course, I'm happy to listen.
Presentationen var tydlig, men strukturen kunde vara mer kompakt.	The presentation was clear, but the structure could be tighter.
Kan du utveckla det?	Could you elaborate?
Vissa delar upprepades, vilket försvagade effekten.	Some points repeated, which weakened the impact.
Jag förstår. Var det något som fungerade särskilt bra?	I see. Was there something that worked especially well?
Inledningen var stark och fångade intresset direkt.	The introduction was strong and engaging.
Tack för din ärlighet.	Thank you for your honesty.
Min avsikt är att hjälpa, inte att kritisera.	My intention is to help, not criticize.

Engine 265: Cross-Cultural Discussion

I Finland värderas ofta tystnad i samtal.	In Finland, silence is often valued in conversation.
Det är intressant. I vår kultur kan tystnad kännas obekväm.	That's interesting. In our culture, silence can feel uncomfortable.
Hur påverkar det interaktionen?	How does that affect interaction?
Människor fyller snabbt tystnaden med tal.	People tend to fill silence quickly with speech.
I Finland kan tystnad signalera eftertanke.	In Finland, silence can signal thoughtfulness.
Det förändrar perspektivet helt.	That completely changes the perspective.
Kulturella skillnader kan orsaka missförstånd.	Cultural differences can cause misunderstandings.
Men de kan också berika samtalet.	But they can also enrich conversation.

Engine 266: Conflict De-Escalation

Det känns som att vårt samtal har blivit spänt.	It feels like our conversation has become tense.
Kanske det.	Maybe so.
Kan vi pausa ett ögonblick och klargöra vad vi är oense om?	Can we pause for a moment and clarify what we disagree on?
Det kan hjälpa.	That might help.
För mig är det viktigaste att vi hittar en lösning, inte en vinnare.	What matters most to me is finding a solution, not a winner.
Jag förstår.	I understand.
Kan vi lyssna på varandra utan avbrott?	Could we listen to each other without interruptions?
Det låter rättvist.	That sounds fair.

Tack, jag uppskattar det lugna förhållningssättet.	Thank you, I appreciate the calm approach.

Engine 267: Human–AI Responsibility Conversation

AI kan fatta beslut snabbt, men vem bär ansvaret?	AI can make decisions quickly, but who carries responsibility?
Ansvaret kan inte ligga enbart på systemet.	Responsibility cannot rest solely on the system.
Bör människor alltid granska kritiska beslut?	Should humans always review critical decisions?
Åtminstone när konsekvenserna är betydande.	At least when the consequences are significant.
Vad händer om systemet gör ett misstag?	What if the system makes a mistake?
Då ligger ansvaret hos dem som utformade och implementerade det.	Then responsibility belongs to those who designed and deployed it.
Kan AI öka rättvisan?	Can AI increase fairness?
Ja, om datan är av hög kvalitet och tillsynen god.	Yes, if the data is high-quality and oversight is proper.
Kanske är det viktigaste att bevara mänskligt omdöme.	Perhaps the most important thing is to preserve human judgment.
Precis. Teknik är ett verktyg, inte en moralisk aktör.	Exactly. Technology is a tool, not a moral agent.

Engine 268: Continuing the Conversation

Vi har pratat om många saker.	We have talked about many things.

Ja, det har vi.	We have.
Det känns som att samtalet har förändrats längs vägen.	It feels like the conversation has changed along the way.
Kanske har vi också förändrats.	Maybe we have changed too.
Vad har du lärt dig av dessa samtal?	What have you learned from these conversations?
Att lyssna är viktigare än att vinna.	That listening is more important than winning.
Och att osäkerhet inte är en svaghet.	And that uncertainty is not weakness.
Det är en del av tänkandet.	It is part of thinking.
Fortsätter samtalet härifrån?	Does the conversation continue from here?
Ja. Varje nytt möte är en ny början.	Yes. Every new encounter is a new beginning.
Säg något på svenska.	Say something in Swedish.
Och lyssna noggrant.	And listen carefully.

Engine 269: Natural Conversation Fillers

Nå…	Well… / So…
Ja.	Yeah / Yes
Precis.	Right / Exactly
Jaså?	Oh? / Really?
Aha!	Ah! I see!
Jaså, jag förstår.	I see. / Is that so.
Okej.	Okay / Got it

Sant.	True / That's true
Okej.	Okay
Bra.	Good / Sounds good

Mini Conversation Using Fillers

Jaså? Är du redan här?	Oh? Are you already here?
Ja, jag kom tidigt.	Yeah, I came early.
Aha, okej.	Ah, I see.
Nå… ska vi gå och ta en kaffe?	Well… shall we go for coffee?
Bra idé!	Good idea!
Precis, jag tänkte samma sak.	Right, I thought the same.

Two Very Common Ones

Så ja.	Alright / Okay then
Så där ja!	There we go!

Example:

Swedish	English
Så där ja, nu fungerar det.	There we go, now it works.

Emergency Conversation Tools (Quick Reference)

(You can ask these anytime during a conversation.)

Kan du upprepa?	Can you repeat?

Kan du prata långsammare?	Can you speak more slowly?
Ursäkta, jag förstod inte.	Sorry, I didn't understand.
Vad betyder detta?	What does this mean?
Hur säger man … på svenska?	How do you say … in Swedish?
Jag lär mig svenska.	I'm learning Swedish.
Tack för ditt tålamod.	Thank you for your patience.

Short Intro Line

Ibland i samtal behöver du bara ett litet verktyg för att komma vidare.	Sometimes in conversation you just need a small tool to keep going.

Engine 270: Listener Responses

Precis.	Exactly. / That's right.
Exakt.	Exactly / Precisely
Jaså?	Really? / Is that so?
Jag förstår.	I see. / Is that so.
Sant.	True.
Jag förstår.	I understand.
Okej.	Got it.
Bra att veta.	Good to know.
Låter bra.	Sounds good.
Det kan vara så.	Could be. / Possibly.

Mini Listening Conversation

Jag flyttade till Helsingfors förra året.	I moved to Helsinki last year.
Jaså?	Oh really?
Ja, på grund av mitt arbete.	Yes, because of my job.
Jag förstår, precis.	I see, I understand.
Det har varit ett bra beslut.	It has been a good decision.
Precis, det låter bra.	Exactly, that sounds good.

Very Natural Listening Loop

Exakt. Right.

Precis. Exactly.

Jag förstår. I see.

Jag förstår. I understand.

Engine 271: Thinking Words

Nå, alltså…	Well… / Let me think…
Öh…	Uh…
Vänta lite…	One moment…
Vi får se…	Let's see…
Hmm…	Hmm…
Kanske…	Maybe…
Jag vet inte…	I don't know…

Svårt att säga…	Hard to say…
Jag tror att…	I think that…
Det kan vara så att…	It might be that…

Mini Thinking Conversation

Var vill du äta idag?	Where do you want to eat today?
Hmm… vi får se…	Hmm… let's see…
Kanske en italiensk restaurang?	Maybe an Italian restaurant?
Bra idé.	Good idea.
Nå, alltså… känner du till ett bra ställe?	Well… do you know a good place?
Jag tror att jag känner till ett.	I think I know one.

Natural Thinking Loop

Nå, alltså… vi får se… kanske…	Well… let's see… maybe…
Hmm… svårt att säga.	Hmm… hard to say.

Engine 272: Softening Your Opinion

Enligt mig…	In my opinion…
Jag tycker att…	In my opinion…
Jag tror att…	I think that…
Kanske…	Maybe…
Det kan vara så att…	It may be that…

Det kan hända att…	It might be that…
Förmodligen…	Probably…
Jag är inte säker, men…	I'm not sure, but…
Det känns som att…	It feels like…
Det verkar som att…	It looks like…

Mini Conversation Using Soft Opinions

Tycker du om den här restaurangen?	Do you like this restaurant?
Enligt mig är den bra.	In my opinion it is good.
Jag tror att maten är färsk.	I think the food is fresh.
Kanske kan vi komma hit igen.	Maybe we can come here again.
Förmodligen.	Probably.

Natural Opinion Flow

Enligt mig fungerar detta bra.	In my opinion this works well.
Kanske kan vi prova det.	Maybe we can try it.
Det kan vara så att det hjälper.	It may be that it helps.

Engine 273: Agreeing and Disagreeing Politely

Jag håller med.	I agree.
Jag också.	Me too.
Exakt.	Exactly.

Det är sant.	That is true.
Kanske.	Maybe.
Det kan vara så.	Could be.
Jag är inte säker.	I'm not sure.
Jag håller inte riktigt med.	I don't really agree.
Kanske, men…	Maybe, but…
Å andra sidan…	On the other hand…

Mini Conversation

Det här kaféet är det bästa i staden.	This café is the best in the city.
Kanske, men priserna är höga.	Maybe, but the prices are high.
Det är sant.	That is true.
Å andra sidan är kaffet verkligen gott.	On the other hand the coffee is really good.
Jag tycker det också.	I think so too.

Simple Agreement Loop

Det är en bra idé.	That is a good idea.
Jag håller med.	I agree.
Exakt.	Exactly.

Gentle Disagreement

Kanske, men jag är inte säker.	Maybe, but I'm not sure.
Jag håller inte riktigt med.	I don't really agree.

Engine 274: Conversation Extenders

Berätta mer.	Tell me more.
Vad hände sedan?	What happened then?
Hur menar du?	How so?
Varför då?	Why is that?
Och sedan?	And then?
Verkligen?	Really?
Jaså?	Oh really?
Hur kändes det?	How did that feel?
Vad tycker du om det?	What do you think about that?
Det låter intressant.	That sounds interesting.

Mini Conversation Using Extenders

Jag besökte Lappland förra vintern.	I visited Lapland last winter.
Jaså? Berätta mer.	Oh really? Tell me more.
Det var verkligen vackert där.	It was really beautiful there.
Verkligen? Vad hände sedan?	Really? What happened then?
Jag såg norrsken för första gången.	I saw the northern lights for the first time.
Det låter intressant.	That sounds interesting.

Simple Conversation Loop

Berätta mer.	Tell me more.
Jaså?	Oh really?
Hur menar du?	How so?
Och sedan?	And then?

Engine 275: Essential Everyday Phrases

1. Start of the Day — Greetings

Hej. Trevligt att träffas.	Hello. Nice to meet you.
God morgon!	Good morning!
God dag.	Good day.
God kväll.	Good evening.
Hur sov du?	How did you sleep?
Vad ska du göra idag?	What are your plans today?
Behöver du något?	Do you need anything?
Ska vi börja?	Shall we get started?

Mini Conversation Loop

God morgon!	Good morning!
God morgon! Hur sov du?	Good morning! How did you sleep?
Ganska bra, tack. Och du?	Pretty well, thanks. And you?
Bra också. Ska vi börja?	Good as well. Shall we start?

2. Everyday Social Connection

Ursäkta. Jag är ledsen.	Excuse me. I'm sorry.
Hur går det?	How's it going?
Hur mår du idag?	How are you today?
Hur känner du dig?	How do you feel?
Berätta mer!	Tell me more!
Låter bra.	Sounds good.
Jag förstår. Jag förstår inte.	I understand. I don't understand.
Jag är inte säker. Jag är säker.	I'm not sure. I'm sure.
Kan jag hjälpa?	Can I help?
Tack. Nej tack.	Thank you. No thank you.
Ingen orsak.	You're welcome.
Trevligt att prata med dig.	Nice talking with you.

3. Daily Needs & Practical Life

Var är …?	Where is … ?
Kan du visa?	Can you show me?
Får jag använda detta?	Can I use this?
Jag behöver hjälp.	I need help.
Ett ögonblick.	One moment.
Vänta lite.	Wait a moment.
Är detta rätt?	Is this correct?

Hur fungerar detta?	How does this work?
Kan jag få mer?	Can I have more?
Har du tid?	Do you have time?
Ska vi börja nu?	Shall we start now?

4. Food, Coffee, and Daily Eating

Kaffe, tack.	Coffee please.
Vatten, tack.	Water please.
Jag skulle vilja ha denna.	I'd like this one.
Kan jag få vatten?	Could I get some water?
Är detta gott?	Is this good?
Vad är din favorit?	What's your favorite?
Det här är utsökt!	This is delicious!
Kan vi sitta här?	Can we sit here?
Kan jag få notan?	May I have the bill?

5. Ending Interaction

Tack för idag.	Thanks for today.
Vi ses snart.	See you soon.
Vi ses senare.	See you later.
Ha en trevlig kväll.	Have a good evening.
God natt.	Good night.

Kontakta mig imorgon.	Contact me tomorrow.
Vi pratar senare.	Let's talk later.
Hej då.	Goodbye.
Hej hej.	Bye-bye.
Adjö.	Goodbye.
Ha en fortsatt trevlig dag.	Have a nice rest of the day.

Engine 276: Starter, Follow-up, Deepen, Close Builder

Engine 276 fungerar som en flexibel ingångspunkt i samtal.	Engine 276 serves as a flexible entry point into conversations.
Den kopplar till alla andra engines (1–287) och kan användas för att börja, förlänga eller återuppta en dialog.	It connects to all other engines (1–287) and can be used to begin, extend, or restart a dialogue.
Denna engine fungerar som ett Guidat Öppet Loop-system för samtal, där inläraren aktivt bygger samtalet steg för steg.	This engine operates as a Guided Open Loop Conversation System, where the learner actively builds the conversation step by step.
Du kan:	You may:
• Svara fritt med egna ord	• Respond freely in your own words
• Använda delar från Starter, Follow-up, Deepen eller Close	• Use elements from Starter, Follow-up, Deepen, or Close engines
• Kombinera mönster för att utveckla ett komplett samtal	• Combine patterns to develop a complete conversation
Det finns inget enda korrekt svar.	There is no single correct answer.
Varje svar skapar en ny väg framåt.	Each response creates a new path forward.
Målet är enkelt:	The objective is simple:

engagera, reflektera och fortsätta.	engage, reflect, and continue.

Starter (Reflektio)

Jag har funderat på något du sa tidigare.	I've been thinking about something you said earlier.
Jag skulle vilja återkomma till en sak en stund.	There's something I'd like to revisit for a moment.
Jag är inte helt säker på hur jag ska formulera detta, men jag försöker.	I'm not entirely sure how to frame this, but let me try.
Det här kan vara ett lite annorlunda perspektiv, men lyssna en stund.	This might be a slightly different angle, but hear me out.
Jag skulle vilja undersöka detta lite mer noggrant.	I'd like to explore this a bit more carefully.
Något i detta känns inte helt rätt för mig.	Something about this doesn't sit quite right with me.
Jag tror att vi ser på detta från olika perspektiv.	I think we might be looking at this from different perspectives.
Låt mig pausa här och reflektera en stund.	Let me pause here and reflect on that for a second.
Jag skulle vilja förstå detta tydligare innan vi går vidare.	I'd like to understand this more clearly before we move on.
Det här väcker en intressant fråga för mig.	This raises an interesting question for me.
Jag är nyfiken på hur du ser på detta just nu.	I'm curious how you're seeing this right now.
Jag vill närma mig detta eftertänksamt, inte reaktivt.	I want to approach this thoughtfully rather than reactively.

Det finns en nyans här som jag inte vill missa.	There's a nuance here that I don't want to miss.
Jag kan ha fel, men så här uppfattar jag det.	I may be wrong, but this is how it's coming across to me.
Låt oss ta ett steg tillbaka och se helheten.	Let's take a step back and look at the bigger picture.
Jag tror att det finns mer här än det först verkar.	I think there's more underneath this than it first appears.
Jag skulle vilja sakta ner detta lite så att vi verkligen förstår det.	I'd like to slow this down just enough to understand it properly.
Det här känns som ett viktigt tillfälle att klargöra saker.	This feels like an important moment to clarify things.
Jag märker något här som kan vara värt att utforska.	I'm noticing something that might be worth exploring.
Innan vi går vidare, kan vi säkerställa en sak?	Before we go further, can we align on one point?
Jag skulle vilja återvända till avsikten bakom detta.	I'd like to revisit the intention behind this.
Det här förtjänar en närmare granskning.	Something about this deserves a closer look.
Jag tror att vi kan vara inne på något djupare här.	I think we may be touching on something deeper here.
Låt mig kontrollera att jag förstår detta korrekt.	Let me check that I'm understanding this correctly.
Jag skulle vilja bidra med ett lite annorlunda perspektiv.	I'd like to bring a slightly different perspective into this.
Det här känns mer komplext än det först verkade.	This feels more complex than it first seemed.
Jag skulle vilja bryta ner detta lite.	I'd like to unpack this a bit.

Jag känner att det finns mer bakom detta än vi har sagt.	I'm sensing there's more behind this than we've said.
Kan vi pausa och titta på detta från en annan vinkel?	Can we pause and look at this from another angle?
Jag vill vara försiktig så att vi inte förenklar detta för mycket.	I want to be careful not to oversimplify this.
Jag skulle vilja förstå vad som verkligen driver detta.	I'd like to understand what's really driving this.
Det finns en del här som jag skulle vilja förtydliga.	There's a part of this I'd like to clarify.
Låt mig låta detta sjunka in en stund.	Let me sit with that for a moment.
Jag tror att vi börjar närma oss kärnan nu.	I think we may be approaching the core of it now.
Jag skulle vilja närma mig detta med lite mer precision.	I'd like to approach this with a bit more precision.
Det finns något här som jag inte vill gå förbi för snabbt.	There's something here that I don't want to rush past.
Jag vill säkerställa att vi inte missar något viktigt.	I want to make sure we're not missing something important.
Låt oss ta en stund och strukturera detta.	Let's take a moment to ground this.
Jag är intresserad av vad detta faktiskt betyder i praktiken.	I'm interested in what this really means in practice.
Det här känns som ett bra ställe att pausa och reflektera.	This seems like a good place to pause and reflect.
Jag skulle vilja förstå tanken bakom detta.	I'd like to understand the reasoning behind this.
Låt mig omformulera detta lite.	Let me reframe this slightly.
Jag undrar om vi ställer rätt fråga.	I'm wondering if we're asking the right question.

Jag skulle vilja närma mig detta från en annan synvinkel.	I'd like to approach this from a different lens.
Det finns en subtil men viktig punkt här.	There's a subtle point here worth exploring.
Jag tror att detta hänger ihop med något större.	I think this connects to something larger.
Jag skulle vilja spåra detta tillbaka till dess ursprung.	I'd like to trace this back to its source.
Det här kan kräva lite mer noggrant övervägande.	This might require a bit more careful thought.
Låt mig ta ett steg tillbaka innan jag svarar.	Let me take a step back before responding.
Jag skulle vilja börja med en enkel observation.	I'd like to begin with a simple observation.

Starter (Expansion)

Vad har du haft på hjärnan på sistone?	What's been on your mind lately?
Vad har tagit upp det mesta av din uppmärksamhet den senaste tiden?	What has been taking most of your attention these days?
Vad har du funderat på den senaste tiden?	What's something you've been thinking about recently?
Hur har din dag varit hittills?	What kind of day has it been for you so far?
Vad har varit den mest intressanta delen av din vecka?	What's been the most interesting part of your week?
Vad har du fokuserat på den senaste tiden?	What have you been focusing on lately?

Vad har förändrats för dig den senaste tiden?	What's been changing for you recently?
Vad är något som särskilt fastnade hos dig idag?	What's something that stood out to you today?
Vad har tagit upp din tid den senaste tiden?	What's been occupying your time recently?
Vad har du försökt reda ut den senaste tiden?	What's something you've been trying to figure out?
Vad har gått bra för dig den senaste tiden?	What has been going well for you lately?
Vad har varit mer utmanande än du förväntade dig den senaste tiden?	What has been more difficult than expected recently?
Vilken typ av projekt har du varit involverad i den senaste tiden?	What kind of projects have you been involved in lately?
Vad har väckt ditt intresse den senaste tiden?	What has been capturing your interest these days?
Vad har du lärt dig den senaste tiden?	What have you been learning recently?
Vad har varit annorlunda med den här veckan jämfört med vanligt?	What's been different about this week compared to usual?
Vad är något du har tänkt återvända till men ännu inte hunnit?	What's something you've been meaning to get back to?
Vad har motiverat dig den senaste tiden?	What's been motivating you lately?
Vad har överraskat dig den senaste tiden?	What's something that surprised you recently?
Vad har hållit dig lagom sysselsatt på sistone?	What's been keeping you busy in a good way?
Vad har varit på din radar den senaste tiden?	What's been on your radar recently?

Vilken typ av saker har du utforskat den senaste tiden?	What kind of things have you been exploring lately?
Vad har börjat ta form för dig den senaste tiden?	What's been taking shape for you recently?
Vad är något du har återvänt till eller tänkt om kring?	What's something you've been revisiting or rethinking?
Vad har gett dig energi den senaste tiden?	What's been giving you energy lately?
Vad har tagit din energi den senaste tiden?	What's been draining your energy lately?
Vad är något som har varit under utveckling för dig den senaste tiden?	What's something that's been evolving for you?
Vad är något du gradvis har förbättrat den senaste tiden?	What's something you've been gradually improving?
Vad har varit viktigare för dig den senaste tiden än tidigare?	What's been more important to you recently than before?
Vad är något du har uppmärksammat mer noggrant den senaste tiden?	What's something you've been paying closer attention to?
Vilken typ av samtal har du haft den senaste tiden?	What kind of conversations have you been having lately?
Vad är något som har varit mer i ditt huvud än vanligt den senaste tiden?	What's something that's been on your mind more than usual?
Vad har du varit nyfiken på den senaste tiden?	What's something you've been curious about recently?
Hur har dina prioriteringar förändrats den senaste tiden?	What's been shifting in your priorities lately?
Vad har du försökt förstå bättre den senaste tiden?	What's something you've been trying to understand better?
Vad har du byggt eller utvecklat den senaste tiden?	What's something you've been building or developing?

Vad har utmanat dig på ett konstruktivt sätt?	What's been challenging you in a productive way?
Vad är något du har arbetat dig igenom den senaste tiden?	What's something you've been working through recently?
Vad är något du medvetet har förändrat den senaste tiden?	What's something you've been intentionally changing?
Vad är något som gradvis har öppnat sig för dig?	What's something that's been unfolding for you?
Vad är något som har blivit tydligare för dig den senaste tiden?	What's something that's been clearer to you lately?
Vad är något du har justerat eller finjusterat den senaste tiden?	What's something you've been adjusting or refining?
Vad är något du har blivit mer medveten om den senaste tiden?	What's something you've been more aware of recently?
Vad är något som har börjat falla på plats för dig den senaste tiden?	What's something that's been coming together for you?
Vad är något du har experimenterat med den senaste tiden?	What's something you've been experimenting with?
Vad är något du har närmat dig på ett annat sätt den senaste tiden?	What's something you've been approaching differently?
Vad är något du har märkt oftare den senaste tiden?	What's something you've been noticing more often?
Vad är något du har försökt förenkla den senaste tiden?	What's something you've been trying to simplify?
Vad är något du har prioriterat mer noggrant den senaste tiden?	What's something you've been prioritizing more carefully?
Vad är något som har varit värt din uppmärksamhet den senaste tiden?	What's something that's been worth your attention lately?

Follow-Up

Vad är det som står ut mest för dig i den situationen?	What stands out most to you in that situation?
Hur kom du fram till den slutsatsen?	How did you arrive at that conclusion?
Vad påverkade ditt sätt att tänka där?	What influenced your thinking there?
Kan du gå igenom din tankekedja?	Can you walk me through your reasoning?
Vilken del känns mest betydelsefull för dig?	What part of that feels most significant to you?
Hur tolkar du det nu?	How do you interpret that now?
Vad förändrade ditt perspektiv?	What changed your perspective?
Vad tror du driver detta?	What do you think is driving that?
Hur hänger detta ihop med din tidigare tanke?	How does that connect to your earlier point?
Vad skulle du säga är den viktigaste faktorn här?	What would you say is the key factor here?
Hur ser du att detta utvecklas?	How do you see this evolving?
Vad gör detta särskilt viktigt för dig?	What makes this particularly important to you?
Vad väger du in i det här beslutet?	What are you weighing in that decision?
Hur stämmer detta överens med dina förväntningar?	How does this align with what you expected?
Vad skulle du göra annorlunda nu?	What would you do differently now?
Vad är din känsla för vart detta är på väg?	What's your sense of where this is heading?
Hur påverkade det ditt sätt att tänka?	How did that affect your thinking?

Vad känns fortfarande olöst för dig?	What feels unresolved for you?
Vad är den underliggande oron här?	What's the underlying concern here?
Vad säger din intuition dig?	What's your intuition telling you?
Hur skiljer du mellan alternativen?	How do you distinguish between the options?
Vad känns mest osäkert just nu?	What feels most uncertain right now?
Vad skulle göra detta tydligare för dig?	What would clarify this for you?
Hur definierar du framgång i den här situationen?	How do you define success in this situation?
Vad prioriterar du här?	What are you prioritizing here?
Vilka antaganden kan påverka detta?	What assumptions might be shaping this?
Hur jämför sig detta med dina tidigare erfarenheter?	How does this compare to past experiences?
Vad märker du när du reflekterar över detta?	What are you noticing as you reflect on it?
Vad skulle förändra ditt perspektiv?	What would shift your perspective?
Hur passar detta in i helheten?	How does this fit into the bigger picture?
Vad känns mest relevant just nu?	What feels most relevant right now?
Vad är fortfarande oklart för dig?	What's still unclear to you?
Hur skulle du förklara detta för någon annan?	How would you explain this to someone else?
Vad känns konsekvent och vad gör det inte?	What feels consistent, and what doesn't?
Vad är din nuvarande tolkning av detta?	What's your current interpretation?

Vad är den mest meningsfulla insikten för dig här?	What's the most meaningful takeaway for you?
Vad påverkar din reaktion?	What's influencing your reaction?
Hur utvärderar du det resultatet?	How do you evaluate that outcome?
Vad är viktigast i detta sammanhang?	What matters most in this context?
Vad är din nuvarande tankelinje?	What's your current line of thinking?
Hur balanserar du dessa faktorer?	How do you balance those factors?
Vad känns mest stabilt för dig?	What feels most grounded to you?
Vad håller du fast vid här?	What are you holding onto here?
Vad skulle utmana din nuvarande syn?	What would challenge your current view?
Vilket perspektiv kan saknas?	What perspective might be missing?
Hur får du detta att gå ihop för dig själv?	How do you make sense of that?
Vad skulle du behöva för att känna dig säker på detta?	What would you need to feel confident about this?
Vad känns mest i linje med dig?	What feels most aligned for you?
Hur tolkar du det resultatet nu?	How do you interpret that outcome now?
Vilken riktning antyder detta för dig?	What direction does this suggest to you?

Follow-Up (Expansion)

Vad gjorde det särskilt betydelsefullt för dig?	What made that stand out to you?
Hur utvecklades situationen över tid?	How did that situation develop over time?

Vad ledde dig till den slutsatsen?	What led you to that conclusion?
Vilken del av det har varit mest meningsfull?	What part of that has been the most meaningful?
Vad gjorde det mer utmanande än du förväntade dig?	What made that more challenging than expected?
Hur närmade du dig det i början?	How did you approach it at the beginning?
Vad förändrades längs vägen?	What changed along the way?
Vad fick dig att besluta att hantera det på det sättet?	What made you decide to handle it that way?
Vilka faktorer påverkade ditt beslut mest?	What factors influenced your decision most?
Vad gjorde den erfarenheten annorlunda jämfört med andra?	What made that experience different from others?
Vad märkte du när saker och ting utvecklades?	What did you notice as things progressed?
Vad märkte du att du lade märke till?	What did you find yourself paying attention to?
Vilken del krävde mest ansträngning?	What part of it required the most effort?
Vad visade sig vara lättare än du förväntade dig?	What did you find easier than expected?
Vad lärde du dig av den processen?	What did you learn from that process?
Vad gjorde situationen mer komplex?	What made that situation more complex?
Vad hjälpte dig att gå vidare?	What helped you move forward?
Vad bromsade din framgång?	What slowed things down for you?

Vad behövde du justera längs vägen?	What did you have to adjust along the way?
Vad gjorde det resultatet möjligt?	What made that outcome possible?
Vilken del av det överraskade dig mest?	What part of it surprised you the most?
Vilka antaganden utgick du ifrån?	What assumptions did you start with?
Vad förändrade ditt perspektiv?	What changed your perspective?
Vad fick dig att ompröva din strategi?	What made you reconsider your approach?
Vad märkte du att du ifrågasatte?	What did you find yourself questioning?
Vad gjorde beslutet tydligare?	What made that decision clearer?
Vad gjorde det svårare att fatta beslut?	What made it harder to decide?
Vilken typ av återkoppling fick du?	What kind of feedback did you get?
Vad påverkade ditt tänkande mest?	What influenced your thinking the most?
Vad fick dig att fortsätta?	What made you stick with it?
Vad fick dig att omvärdera din ursprungliga idé?	What made you rethink your initial idea?
Vad kändes mest givande?	What did you find most rewarding?
Vilken del krävde mest tålamod?	What part required the most patience?
Vad gjorde det värt att fortsätta?	What made that worth continuing?
Vad hjälpte dig att vara konsekvent?	What helped you stay consistent?
Vad gjorde det mer hanterbart?	What made that more manageable?
Vad var du tvungen att släppa taget om?	What did you have to let go of?
Vad blev lättare med tiden?	What made that easier over time?

Vad insåg du i efterhand?

What did you realize afterward?

Vilken del skulle du hantera annorlunda nu?

What part would you handle differently now?

Vad gjorde situationen tydligare i efterhand?

What made that situation clearer in hindsight?

Vilken typ av kompromisser var involverade?

What kind of trade-offs were involved?

Vad gjorde det angreppssättet effektivt?

What made that approach effective?

Vad lärde du dig om dig själv genom detta?

What did you learn about yourself from that?

Vad gjorde det ögonblicket betydelsefullt?

What made that moment significant?

Vad gjorde situationen mer nyanserad än den först verkade?

What made that situation more nuanced than it seemed?

Vad hjälpte dig att navigera i osäkerheten?

What helped you navigate that uncertainty?

Vad gjorde upplevelsen värdefull som helhet?

What made that experience valuable overall?

Vad gjorde processen värd ansträngningen?

What made that process worth the effort?

Vad gjorde det särskilt jämfört med liknande erfarenheter?

What made that stand out compared to similar experiences?

Deepen (Reflection / Insight Layer)

Det verkar som att det finns mer under ytan här.

It seems like there's more beneath the surface here.

Detta kan handla mindre om själva situationen och mer om dess innebörd.

This might be less about the situation and more about the meaning behind it.

Ibland pekar det som känns oklart på något viktigt.	Sometimes what feels unclear is actually pointing to something important.
Bakom sådana här stunder finns ofta ett djupare mönster.	There's often a deeper pattern behind moments like this.
Det som är betydelsefullt är inte bara vad som hände, utan hur det påverkade dig.	What stands out isn't just what happened, but how it affected you.
Detta kan vara en möjlighet att förstå något mer grundläggande.	This could be an opportunity to understand something more fundamental.
Spänningen här kan avslöja något värt att uppmärksamma.	The tension here might be revealing something worth paying attention to.
Det du beskriver tyder på en förändring i perspektiv.	What you're describing suggests a shift in perspective.
Det verkar som att detta hänger ihop med något större.	It sounds like this connects to something broader.
Det kan finnas mer än en sanning här samtidigt.	There may be more than one truth present here.
Detta verkar spegla en djupare inre process.	This seems to reflect a deeper internal process.
Ibland uppstår klarhet genom att vara kvar i osäkerheten.	Sometimes clarity comes from sitting with the uncertainty.
Det som känns olöst bär ofta på värdefull insikt.	What feels unresolved often carries useful insight.
Det handlar kanske mindre om att hitta ett svar och mer om att ställa bättre frågor.	This may be less about finding an answer and more about asking better questions.
Det finns en skillnad mellan att reagera och att förstå.	There's a difference between reacting and understanding.

Det du märker kan peka mot ett större mönster.	What you're noticing may point to a larger pattern.
Det kan hjälpa att skilja på vad som hände och hur det upplevdes.	It might help to separate what happened from how it was experienced.
Detta kan vara ett tillfälle för omkalibrering.	This could be a moment of recalibration.
Det finns ofta mening i det vi tvekar att säga högt.	There's often meaning in what we hesitate to say.
Detta kan vara en inbjudan att titta närmare.	This might be an invitation to look more closely.
Ibland gör avstånd att strukturen blir tydligare.	Sometimes stepping back reveals the structure more clearly.
Det känns som en vändpunkt i hur du ser på saker.	This feels like a turning point in how you're seeing things.
Den här komplexiteten kan vara nödvändig, inte slumpmässig.	The complexity here might be necessary, not accidental.
Det som håller på att träda fram kan ta tid att förstå.	What's emerging may take time to fully understand.
Detta kanske inte behöver lösas direkt.	This may not need to be resolved immediately.
Det finns värde i att stanna kvar i frågan lite längre.	There's value in staying with the question a bit longer.
Det kan handla mindre om säkerhet och mer om medvetenhet.	This could be less about certainty and more about awareness.
Det du beskriver bär på en stillsam klarhet.	What you're describing carries a kind of quiet clarity.
Insikt uppstår ofta gradvis, inte på en gång.	Sometimes insight comes gradually rather than all at once.

Detta kan avslöja något om dina prioriteringar.	This might be revealing something about your priorities.
Under det som verkar oklart finns ofta en inre logik.	There's often coherence beneath apparent confusion.
Detta kan peka mot en djupare linjering.	This could be pointing toward a deeper alignment.
Sättet du formulerar detta på förändrar det redan.	The way you're framing this is already shifting it.
Här finns en subtil men viktig skillnad.	There's a subtle distinction here that matters.
Detta kan vara mer sammanlänkat än det först verkar.	This may be more interconnected than it appears.
Det som känns svårt rymmer ofta mest insikt.	What feels difficult often holds the most insight.
Detta kan vara en del av en större förändring.	This might be part of a larger transition.
Det finns en typ av klarhet som bara kommer genom reflektion.	There's a kind of clarity that only comes through reflection.
Det handlar kanske mindre om att lösa och mer om att se tydligt.	This may be less about solving and more about seeing clearly.
Det som nu blir synligt var kanske inte det tidigare.	What's becoming visible now may not have been before.
Detta kan vara en möjlighet att förfina ditt sätt att närma dig detta.	This could be an opportunity to refine how you approach this.
Det finns mening i hur detta utvecklas.	There's meaning in the way this is unfolding.
Det du märker nu kan förändra hur du går vidare.	What you're noticing might reshape how you move forward.
Detta kan vara ett tillfälle att ompröva antaganden.	This might be a moment to reconsider assumptions.

Insikt uppstår ofta i pauserna mellan slutsatser.	There's often insight in the pauses between conclusions.
Detta kan peka mot ett annat sätt att engagera sig i detta.	This could be pointing toward a different way of engaging.
Själva processen kan vara viktigare än resultatet.	The process itself may be more important than the outcome.
Detta verkar bära på en djupare form av sammanhang.	This seems to carry a deeper kind of coherence.
Det kan finnas värde i att inte skynda fram till en slutsats.	There may be value in not rushing to closure.
Det som håller på att framträda kan bli tydligare med tiden.	What's emerging here may become clearer with time.

Deepen (Expansion)

Hur brukar du vanligtvis utvärdera sådana situationer?	How do you usually evaluate situations like that?
Vilka återkommande mönster har du börjat lägga märke till?	What patterns have you started to notice?
Hur har ditt perspektiv förändrats över tid?	How has your perspective changed over time?
Vad säger den erfarenheten om dina prioriteringar?	What does that experience say about your priorities?
Hur brukar du avgöra vad som är viktigast?	How do you usually decide what matters most?
Vad tror du påverkade ditt tänkande mest?	What do you think influenced your thinking the most?
Hur tolkar du det resultatet nu?	How do you interpret that outcome now?

Vad avslöjar detta om hur du närmar dig saker?

What does that reveal about how you approach things?

Hur brukar du hantera osäkerhet i sådana situationer?

How do you usually respond to uncertainty like that?

Vad antyder den erfarenheten om dina mål?

What does that experience suggest about your goals?

Hur balanserar du motstridiga prioriteringar i sådana situationer?

How do you balance competing priorities in situations like that?

Vilket slags tänkande hjälpte dig mest i den situationen?

What kind of thinking helped you most there?

Vilka principer vägledde ditt beslut?

What principles guided your decision?

Vilka kompromisser behövde du acceptera?

What trade-offs did you have to accept?

Hur brukar du mäta framsteg i sådana situationer?

How do you usually measure progress in situations like that?

Hur ser framgång ut för dig i det sammanhanget?

What does success look like to you in that context?

Vad gjorde situationen mer komplex än den först verkade?

What made that situation more complex than it appeared?

Vad tror du gjorde den största skillnaden?

What do you think made the biggest difference?

Hur brukar du reflektera över sådana erfarenheter?

How do you usually reflect on experiences like that?

Vad skulle du betrakta som den viktigaste lärdomen?

What would you consider the key takeaway?

Hur skiljer du mellan kortsiktigt och långsiktigt värde i en sådan situation?

How do you distinguish between short-term and long-term value there?

Vad skulle du göra annorlunda i samma situation nu?

What would you do differently with the same situation now?

Vilket slags tankesätt hjälpte dig mest?	What kind of mindset helped you most?
Vad utmanade dina antaganden mest?	What challenged your assumptions the most?
Vad gjorde erfarenheten meningsfull utöver resultatet?	What made that experience meaningful beyond the outcome?
Hur brukar du bearbeta sådana erfarenheter i efterhand?	How do you usually process experiences like that afterward?
Vad skulle du vilja utforska djupare baserat på detta?	What would you want to explore further based on that?
Vad avslöjar den här situationen om ditt beslutsfattande?	What does that situation reveal about your decision-making?
Hur anpassar du dig när saker inte går som förväntat?	How do you adapt when things don't go as expected?
Vad tycker du är viktigast i sådana situationer?	What do you think matters most in situations like that?
Hur avgör du om något var värt ansträngningen?	How do you evaluate whether something was worth the effort?
Vad gjorde situationen värd att reflektera över?	What made that situation worth reflecting on?
Vad skulle du ta med dig vidare från den erfarenheten?	What would you carry forward from that experience?
Vad påverkade din tolkning av resultatet?	What influenced your interpretation of the outcome?
Hur närmar du dig liknande utmaningar nu?	How do you usually approach similar challenges now?
Vilken typ av utveckling kom ur den erfarenheten?	What kind of growth came from that experience?
Vad klargjorde den erfarenheten för dig?	What did that experience clarify for you?

Vad tror du formade din reaktion mest?	What do you think shaped your response the most?
Hur skulle du närma dig detta annorlunda nästa gång?	What would you approach differently next time?
Vad lärde den erfarenheten dig om ditt eget arbetssätt?	What did that experience teach you about your own process?
Hur avgör du när du ska fortsätta och när du ska byta riktning?	How do you decide when to persist versus change direction?
Vilken typ av insikter kom ur den erfarenheten?	What kind of insight came out of that experience?
Vad gjorde situationen meningsfull i efterhand?	What made that situation meaningful in hindsight?
Vad säger detta om hur du förhåller dig till förändring?	What does that suggest about how you approach change?
Vilken typ av medvetenhet kom ur den erfarenheten?	What kind of awareness came from that experience?
Vad skulle du vilja förstå djupare om detta?	What would you want to understand more deeply about it?
Vad avslöjar detta om din långsiktiga riktning?	What does that reveal about your long-term direction?
Vilken typ av klarhet kom ur den situationen?	What kind of clarity came from that situation?
Vad tror du var vändpunkten?	What do you think was the turning point?
Vad gjorde att den erfarenheten stannade kvar hos dig?	What made that experience stay with you?

Close (Wrap-Up Engine)

Det ger mig en tydligare bild av var detta står.	That gives me a clearer sense of where this stands.
Jag uppskattar hur du har tänkt igenom detta.	I appreciate the way you've thought this through.
Detta känns som ett meningsfullt steg framåt.	This feels like a meaningful step forward.
Jag tror att vi har nått en användbar nivå av klarhet här.	I think we've reached a useful level of clarity here.
Detta ger oss något stabilt att bygga vidare på.	This gives us something solid to build on.
Jag är glad att vi tog oss tid att utforska detta.	I'm glad we took the time to explore this.
Detta hjälper att få saker i bättre fokus.	This helps bring things into better focus.
Jag känner mig mer i linje med detta efter samtalet.	I feel more aligned after this conversation.
Det var hjälpsamt att arbeta igenom detta tillsammans.	That was helpful to work through together.
Detta känns som ett bra ställe att pausa.	This feels like a good place to pause.
Jag tror att vi har identifierat det viktigaste här.	I think we've uncovered what matters most here.
Detta ger oss en tydligare riktning framåt.	This gives us a clearer direction moving forward.
Jag uppskattar djupet i denna diskussion.	I appreciate the depth of this discussion.
Detta har varit ett värdefullt utbyte.	This has been a valuable exchange.
Jag tror att vi har klargjort kärnan i detta.	I think we've clarified the core of it.
Det ger en känsla av avslutning i detta.	That brings a sense of resolution to this.

Det känns som att vi har gjort detta rättvisa.	I feel like we've done this justice.
Detta ger mig förtroende för nästa steg.	This gives me confidence in the next step.
Jag är bekväm med var vi har landat.	I'm comfortable with where we've landed.
Detta känns som en naturlig avslutningspunkt.	This feels like a natural stopping point.
Jag tror att vi har fört detta framåt på ett meningsfullt sätt.	I think we've moved this forward meaningfully.
Detta har hjälpt att få saker i linje.	This has helped bring things into alignment.
Jag uppskattar din öppenhet i detta.	I appreciate your openness in this.
Det ger ytterligare klarhet i situationen.	That adds clarity to the situation.
Jag tror att vi har nått en gemensam förståelse.	I think we've reached a shared understanding.
Detta känns färdigt för nu.	This feels complete for now.
Jag är glad att vi stannade vid detta tillräckligt länge.	I'm glad we stayed with this long enough.
Detta ger en starkare grund.	That gives this a stronger foundation.
Jag tycker att vi har gjort goda framsteg här.	I think we've made good progress here.
Detta lämnar mig med ett tydligare perspektiv.	This leaves me with a clearer perspective.
Jag uppskattar eftertänksamheten du bidrog med här.	I appreciate the thoughtfulness you brought to this.
Detta har varit värt tiden.	This has been worth the time.

Jag tror att vi har nått något meningsfullt.	I think we've arrived at something meaningful.
Detta ger oss en bra punkt att fortsätta från senare.	This gives us a good point to continue from later.
Jag känner mig lugn med detta nu.	I feel settled about this now.
Detta hjälper att knyta ihop allt.	That helps bring everything together.
Detta klargjorde mer än jag förväntade mig.	This has clarified more than I expected.
Jag tror att vi har nått en balanserad syn.	I think we've reached a balanced view.
Detta ger oss tillräcklig klarhet för nu.	This gives us enough clarity for now.
Jag uppskattar hur detta utvecklades.	I appreciate how this unfolded.
Detta känns välgrundat och genomtänkt.	This feels grounded and considered.
Jag tror att vi har utforskat detta grundligt.	I think we've explored this thoroughly.
Detta ger oss något att ta med oss vidare.	This gives us something to carry forward.
Jag känner mig nöjd med var vi har landat.	I feel good about where we've landed.
Det ger en känsla av avslutning i detta skede.	That brings a sense of closure to this part.
Detta har varit en konstruktiv diskussion.	This has been a constructive conversation.
Jag tror att vi har fångat de viktigaste punkterna.	I think we've captured the key points.
Detta ger oss en tydlig fortsättningspunkt.	This gives us a clear place to continue from.

Jag är nöjd med riktningen detta har tagit.	I'm satisfied with the direction this has taken.
Detta känns som en genomtänkt slutsats.	This feels like a thoughtful conclusion.

Close (Expansion)

Det ger mig mycket att tänka på — tack för att du delade detta.	That gives me a lot to think about—thanks for sharing.
Jag uppskattar hur du förklarade det — det är logiskt.	I appreciate how you explained that—it makes sense.
Det är ett hjälpsamt sätt att se på det.	That's a helpful way to look at it.
Jag hade inte tänkt på det så tidigare.	I hadn't thought about it that way before.
Det ger mycket klarhet — tack.	That adds a lot of clarity—thank you.
Det var verkligen intressant att höra.	That was really interesting to hear.
Jag är glad att vi pratade om det.	I'm glad we talked about that.
Det var ett värdefullt perspektiv.	That was a valuable perspective.
Det gav mig en ny vinkel att överväga.	That gave me a new angle to consider.
Jag uppskattar djupet i din förklaring.	I appreciate the depth of that explanation.
Det var värt att utforska — tack för att du gick igenom det.	That was worth exploring—thanks for walking through it.
Det hjälpte mig att förstå ditt sätt att tänka bättre.	That helped me understand your thinking better.
Det var en meningsfull konversation.	That was a meaningful conversation.

Det klargjorde mer än jag förväntade mig.	That clarified things more than I expected.
Det var en utmärkt insikt att avsluta med.	That was a great insight to end on.
Det gav mig något användbart att reflektera över.	That gave me something useful to reflect on.
Det knöt ihop helheten på ett bra sätt.	That tied everything together nicely.
Det var en riktigt genomtänkt förklaring.	That was a really thoughtful explanation.
Det gjorde helhetsbilden tydligare.	That made the whole picture clearer.
Det var ett starkt sätt att se på det.	That was a strong way to look at it.
Jag kommer att tänka vidare på det du sa.	I'll think more about what you said.
Det gav mig mycket att reflektera över.	That gave me a lot to reflect on.
Det var ett hjälpsamt sätt att formulera det.	That was a helpful way to frame it.
Jag uppskattar att du tog dig tid att förklara det.	I appreciate you taking the time to explain that.
Det var värt att diskutera.	That was worth the discussion.
Det var ett starkt perspektiv.	That was a solid perspective.
Det tillförde verkligt värde till samtalet.	That added real value to the conversation.
Det hjälpte till att koppla ihop idéerna tydligt.	That helped connect the ideas clearly.
Det gav mig en bättre helhetsförståelse.	That gave me a better understanding overall.
Det var ett användbart sätt att närma sig det.	That was a useful way to approach it.
Det var en bra punkt att avsluta samtalet.	That was a good place to land the conversation.

Det förde allt i tydligt fokus.	That brought everything into focus.
Det var ett genomtänkt sätt att avsluta samtalet.	That was a thoughtful way to wrap it up.
Det hjälpte till att skapa klarhet i diskussionen.	That helped bring clarity to the discussion.
Det gjorde avslutet mer komplett.	That made the conclusion feel complete.
Det var en stark avslutande insikt.	That was a strong closing insight.
Det gav samtalet en tydlig riktning.	That gave the conversation a clear direction.
Det var ett tillfredsställande sätt att avsluta det.	That was a satisfying way to end it.
Det knöt ihop samtalet väl.	That tied the conversation together well.
Det fick diskussionen att kännas komplett.	That made the discussion feel complete.
Det var ett givande utbyte.	That was a worthwhile exchange.
Det var en bra avslutningspunkt.	That was a good note to end on.
Det gav samtalet verkligt djup.	That gave the conversation real depth.
Det var en meningsfull slutsats.	That was a meaningful conclusion.
Det avrundade allt tydligt.	That wrapped things up clearly.
Det fick diskussionen att kännas avslutad.	That made the discussion feel resolved.
Det gav samtalet en stark avslutning.	That gave the conversation a strong finish.
Det var ett tydligt och genomtänkt avslut.	That was a clear and thoughtful ending.

Det lämnade mig med något användbart.	That left me with something useful.
Det var ett utmärkt sätt att avsluta.	That was a great way to conclude.

Engine 277: Standardsvenska vs vardagligt tal

Alla språk har minst två sätt att fungera.
Att förstå båda hjälper dig att lyssna, tala och känna igen riktigt språk.

Standard Swedish (Formell svenska)

Used in:

- books
- news
- official writing
- education

Characteristics:

- full word forms
- clear grammar
- structured sentences

Standardsvenska (formell / skriven)

Används i:
• böcker
• nyheter
• officiella texter
• skola

Egenskaper:
• fullständiga former
• tydlig grammatik
• strukturerade meningar

Svenska	English
Jag är här.	I am here.
Du är min vän.	You are my friend.

Spoken Swedish (Talspråk)

Used in:

- everyday conversation
- informal speech

Characteristics:

- contractions
- relaxed structure
- faster rhythm
- natural flow

Vardagligt tal (talspråk)

Används i:
• samtal
• vänner
• vardagliga situationer

Egenskaper:
• enklare uttal
• naturligt flyt
• mindre formellt

Tal	Standard	English
Ja e här.	Jag är här.	I am here.
Du e min vän.	Du är min vän.	You are my friend.

Samma sak händer i engelska

Standard English	Spoken English
going to	gonna
want to	wanna
you are	you're

Svenska gör samma sak.

Vanliga förenklingar

Tal	Standard	English
ja	jag	I
e	är	am / is
va gör du?	vad gör du?	what are you doing?
de	det	it
dom	de	they

Varför detta är viktigt

Du kommer att:
- läsa standardsvenska
- höra talspråk
- använda båda

Att kunna båda gör samtal enklare och mer naturliga.

Engine 278: Vardagliga verkliga samtal

Detta kapitel visar hur talspråk och standardspråk används tillsammans i riktiga samtal.
Du kommer att känna igen båda — och använda båda.

Vardaglig konversation

Tal	Standard	English
Ja e Mark.	Jag är Mark.	I am Mark.
Du e Alex, eller hur?	Du är Alex, eller hur?	You're Alex, right?
Hur e läget?	Hur är läget?	How are you doing?
Bra, lite upptagen.	Jag mår bra, lite upptagen.	Pretty good, a bit busy.
Var bor du?	Var bor du?	Where do you live?
Ja bor i Stockholm.	Jag bor i Stockholm.	I live in Stockholm.
Var e du ifrån?	Var är du ifrån?	Where are you from?
Ja e från USA.	Jag är från USA.	I'm from the U.S.
Pratar du svenska?	Talar du svenska?	Do you speak Swedish?
Lite, jag lär mig.	Lite, jag lär mig.	Only a little, but I'm learning.
Hur gammal e du?	Hur gammal är du?	How old are you?
Jag e runt trettio.	Jag är runt trettio år.	I'm thirty-ish.

Social konversation

Tal	Standard	English
Ska vi ta en kaffe nån gång?	Ska vi ta en kaffe någon gång?	Shall we go for coffee sometime?
Ja, gärna!	Ja, gärna!	Yeah, let's go!
Har du tid nu?	Har du tid nu?	Do you have time now?
Inte nu, men snart.	Inte nu, men snart.	Not right now, but soon.
Vad gör du imorgon?	Vad gör du imorgon?	What are you doing tomorrow?
Vet inte än.	Jag vet inte än.	I don't know yet.
Vi hörs senare.	Vi hörs senare.	Okay, let's talk later.
Perfekt!	Perfekt!	Works great!

Practice Prompt

Try switching between forms.
Say both versions.
Understanding both helps you listen better and speak naturally.

Tal	Standard
Ja e här.	Jag är här.
Du e här.	Du är här.
Va gör du?	Vad gör du?

Engine 279: Try Other Languages

Language learning begins the moment you are willing to say something.

It does not require perfection, speed, or a large vocabulary.
A single word, a short phrase, or a familiar line is enough.

Say something.
Return to it later.

Language Starters

How would you say **"Say something in another language"**?

Language	Phrase	English
Finnish	**Sano jotain suomeksi.**	Say Something in Finnish.
French	**Dis quelque chose en français.**	Say something in French.
German	**Sag etwas auf Deutsch.**	Say something in German.
Latin	**Dic aliquid Latine.**	Say something in Latin.
Portuguese	**Diga algo em português.**	Say Something in Portuguese.
Spanish	**Di algo en español.**	Say something in Spanish.
Swedish	**Säg något på svenska.**	Say something in Swedish.

French Conversation

French	**English**
Salut ! Comment ta journée a commencé ?	Hi! How has your day started?
Plutôt bien, juste un matin un peu chargé.	Pretty good, just a busy morning.
Ah oui, chargé ? Que s'est-il passé ?	Oh, busy? What happened?
Je me suis réveillé en retard et tout est allé très vite.	I woke up late and everything felt rushed.
Je comprends. Ça t'arrive souvent ?	I get it. Is that common for you?

French	English
Eh, parfois. Mais aujourd'hui, ça me fait déjà rire.	Sometimes. But today I can laugh about it.
Bon à entendre, merci d'avoir partagé.	Good to hear, thanks for sharing.
On continue plus tard !	Let's continue later!

German Conversation

German	English
Hi! Wie hat dein Tag begonnen?	Hi! How has your day started?
Ganz gut, nur ein etwas stressiger Morgen.	Pretty good, just a busy morning.
Oh, stressig? Was ist passiert?	Oh, busy? What happened?
Ich bin zu spät aufgewacht und alles war plötzlich hektisch.	I woke up late and everything felt rushed.
Verstehe. Passiert dir das oft?	I get it. Is that common for you?
Nun, manchmal. Aber heute kann ich schon darüber lachen.	Sometimes, but today I can laugh about it.
Gut zu hören, danke fürs Erzählen.	Good to hear, thanks for sharing.
Wir reden später weiter!	Let's continue later!

Latin Conversation

Latin	English
Salve! Quomodo dies tuus coepit?	Hi! How has your day started?
Satis bene, mane paulum occupato.	Pretty good, just a busy morning.
Heu, occupato? Quid accidit?	Oh, busy? What happened?
Serius evigilavi et omnia festinantia videbantur.	I woke up late and everything felt rushed.

Latin	English
Intellego. Solitumne est tibi?	I get it. Is that common for you?
Interdum, sed hodie iam ridere possum.	Sometimes, but today I can laugh about it.
Bene audire! Gratias quod narrasti.	Good to hear, thanks for sharing.
Postea pergamus!	Let's continue later!

Spanish Conversation

Spanish	English
¡Hola! ¿Cómo empezó tu día?	Hi! How has your day started?
Bastante bien, solo una mañana un poco ocupada.	Pretty good, just a busy morning.
¿Ah sí, ocupada? ¿Qué pasó?	Oh, busy? What happened?
Me desperté tarde y todo fue a las prisas.	I woke up late and everything felt rushed.
Entiendo. ¿Te pasa a menudo?	I get it. Is that common for you?
Bueno, a veces. Pero hoy ya me da risa.	Sometimes. But today I can laugh about it.
Qué bueno, gracias por contarlo.	Good to hear, thanks for sharing.
¡Continuamos más tarde!	Let's continue later!

Swedish Conversation

Swedish	English
Hej! Hur har din dag startat?	Hi! How has your day started?
Ganska bra, bara en lite stressig morgon.	Pretty good, just a busy morning.
Jaså, stressig? Vad hände?	Oh, busy? What happened?

Swedish	English
Jag vaknade sent och allt gick i raketfart.	I woke up late and everything felt rushed.
Förstår. Är det vanligt för dig?	I get it. Is that common for you?
Nja, ibland. Men idag kan jag redan skratta åt det.	Sometimes, but today I can laugh about it.
Bra att höra, tack för att du berättade.	Good to hear, thanks for sharing.
Vi fortsätter senare!	Let's continue later!

Engine 280: The Conversation Toolkit

Svenska	English
Hej! Pratar du engelska eller svenska?	Hi! Do you speak English or Swedish?
Lite av båda. Jag lär mig svenska.	A bit of both. I'm learning Swedish.
Bra! Kan vi prata lite svenska?	Great! Can we speak a little Swedish?
Självklart, men prata lite långsammare.	Of course, but speak a little slower.
Okej. Var kommer du ifrån?	Alright. Where are you from?
Jag kommer från USA. Och du?	I'm from the United States. And you?
Jag kommer från Stockholm.	I'm from Stockholm.
Hur länge har du studerat svenska?	How long have you studied Swedish?
Kanske ungefär sex månader.	Maybe about six months.
Ganska bra! Är svenska svårt?	Pretty good! Is Swedish difficult?
Lite, men det är också intressant.	A little, but it's also interesting.
Ursäkta, kan du upprepa?	Sorry, can you repeat?

Svenska	English
Självklart. Jag sa att svenska är intressant.	Of course. I said Swedish is interesting.
Tack! Vad betyder "intressant"?	Thanks! What does "mielenkiintoista" mean?
Det betyder "interesting".	It means "interesting."
Bra, jag lärde mig ett nytt ord.	Good, I learned a new word.
Har du redan provat en svensk bastu?	Have you tried a Swedish sauna yet?
Ja! Det var väldigt lugnt.	Yes! It was very peaceful.
Jaså? Vad var bäst?	Oh really? What was the best part?
Tystnaden.	The silence.
Det låter väldigt svenskt.	That sounds very Swedish.
Och såklart kaffe efteråt.	And of course coffee afterward.
Sant! I Sverige dricker man mycket kaffe.	True! In Sweden people drink a lot of coffee.
Var finns ett bra café här i närheten?	Where is a good café nearby?
Gå rakt fram och sväng vänster vid hörnet.	Go straight and turn left at the corner.
Tack så mycket!	Thanks a lot!
Förresten, vad är klockan?	By the way, what time is it?
Den är kvart över tre.	It's quarter past three.
Jag kanske går dit nu.	Maybe I'll go there now.
Bra idé.	Good idea.
Om jag inte förstår något, kan jag fråga igen?	If I don't understand something, can I ask again?
Självklart. Fråga gärna.	Of course. Ask freely.

Svenska	English
(en stunds tystnad)	(a moment of silence)
Vet du… i Sverige är även tystnad en del av samtalet.	You know… in Sweden even silence is conversation.
Nåväl. Ska vi ta en kaffe?	Well then. Shall we go for coffee?
Ja, låt oss gå.	Let's go.
Det känns bra.	That feels nice.
Vi fortsätter samtalet på caféet.	Let's continue the conversation at the café.
Det gör vi. Nu går vi.	Let's do that. Let's go.

Engine 281: Flea Circus

Säg något på svenska. Jag såg, färger, loppor, –pa betoning (olipa).	Say something in Swedish. I saw, colors, fleas, –pa emphasis particle (olipa)
Jag hörde att du hade en rolig historia om loppor igår. Låt oss prata om det.	I heard you had a funny story about fleas yesterday. Let's talk about it.
Jag såg en loppcirkus.	I saw a flea circus.
Det fanns många färgade loppor.	There were many colored fleas.
Alla loppor var precis framför mig.	All the fleas were right in front of me.
Fantastiskt, eller hur!	Fantastic, right!
En brun loppa hoppade över bordet.	The brown flea jumped over the table.
En röd loppa hoppade under bordet.	The red flea jumped under the table.

En gul loppa var bredvid det violetta bordet.	The yellow flea was next to the violet table.
En gammal lila loppa var bredvid det nya blå glasbordet.	The old purple flea was next to the new blue glass table.
Men de gröna lopporna hoppade upp på den rosa hunden och var borta på ett ögonblick.	But the green fleas jumped onto the pink dog and were gone in an instant.
Verkligen en intressant föreställning.	Quite an interesting performance indeed.
Vilken färgstark historia!	That was quite a colorful story!
(Det var en färgstark historia.)	(It was a colorful story.) without emphasis.
Tack! Hej då!	Thank you! Bye!

Vocabulary Focus — Colors

Svenska	English	Svenska	English
brun	brown	lila	purple
röd	red	blå	blue
gul	yellow	grön	green
vit	white	svart	black
orange	orange	grå	gray
rosa	pink	ljusbrun	light brown

Grammar Moment

Svenska	English
Låt oss prata om det	"Let's talk about it"

Svenska	English
…eller hur?	confirmation tone ("right?")

Engine 282: Good Study Habits

Tiina, jag funderar på hur jag skulle kunna lära mig språk snabbare.	Tiina, I'm wondering how I could learn Swedish faster.
En hemlighet är att göra små repetitioner varje dag.	One secret is to do small repetitions every day.
Alltså inte för långa pass åt gången?	So not too many long sessions at once?
Precis. Korta men regelbundna stunder är mer effektiva.	Exactly. Short but regular moments are more effective.
Och de där ordbaserade mönstren du pratade om?	And what about those word patterns you talked about?
Ordmönster hjälper dig att komma ihåg grammatik automatiskt.	Word patterns help you remember grammar automatically.
Till exempel "Jag vill …" och jag byter bara ordet i slutet?	For example, "I want …" and just change the word at the end?
Precis! Och när du föreställer dig situationen lär du dig snabbare.	Exactly! And when you imagine the situation, you learn faster.
Så jag använder fantasin – föreställer mig att jag är på ett café eller en station?	So I use my imagination – imagine I'm in a café or at the station?
Ja! Då börjar orden kännas verkliga, inte bara från papper.	Yes! That way the words start to feel real, not just from the paper.
Det här låter till och med roligare än vanlig studietid.	This even sounds more fun than ordinary studying.
Och det är nyckeln: glädje + regelbundenhet = snabbare lärande.	And that's the key: fun + regularity = faster learning.

Engine 283: Selective Word Substitutions

Hej! Hur är läget?	Hi! How's it going?
Hej! [Ganska bra / Rätt bra / Lite trött], tack. Och du?	Hi! [Pretty good / Quite well / A bit tired], thanks. And you?
Tack, jag mår [bra / sådär / ganska stressigt]. Trevligt att se dig.	Thanks, I'm doing [well / so-so / pretty busy]. Nice to see you.
Detsamma! Har du haft en [stressig / lugn / vanlig] dag?	Same here! Have you had a [busy / relaxing / normal] day?
En ganska [vanlig / annorlunda] dag. Hur är vädret där?	A pretty [normal / different] day. How does the weather look there?
Här är det [soligt / regnigt / varmt / kallt]. Och där?	It's [sunny / rainy / warm / cold] here. How about there?
Här är det [blåsigt / molnigt / klart], men det gör inget.	It's [windy / cloudy / clear] here, but I don't mind.
[Regn / Sol / Vind] gör ibland luften [frisk / tung / vacker].	[Rain / Sun / Wind] sometimes makes the air [fresh / heavy / beautiful].
Precis! Får jag fråga var du kommer ifrån?	Exactly! May I ask, where are you from?
Jag kommer från [Stockholm / Göteborg / Malmö / en liten by / ett annat land].	I'm from [Stockholm / Gothenburg / Malmö / a small village / another country].
Låter intressant! Hur är [staden / byn / landet] nuförtiden?	Sounds interesting! What is the [city / village / country] like these days?
Det finns mycket [historia / natur / vackra byggnader / studenter].	There's a lot of [history / nature / beautiful buildings / students].
Fanns det någon särskild [mat / högtid / plats] du tyckte om som barn?	Was there a special [food / celebration / place] you liked as a child?

Ja, jag älskade [potatisgratäng / knäckebröd / lax / choklad].

Yes, I loved [potato casserole / rye bread / salmon / chocolate].

Härligt! Vad gör du på fritiden nu för tiden?

Great! What do you do these days in your free time?

Jag [spelar fotboll / spelar gitarr / läser / ser på film / målar].

I [play football / play guitar / read / watch movies / paint].

Fantastiskt! Vad gör dig [glad / entusiastisk / avslappnad]?

Awesome! What makes you [happy / excited / relaxed]?

[Musik / vänner / sport / natur / familj] gör mig glad.

[Music / friends / sports / nature / family] make me happy.

Jag förstår. Har du några framtidsplaner?

I see. Do you have future plans?

Jag vill [resa / studera / flytta] [till Spanien / till Japan / utomlands / till en ny stad].

I want to [travel / study / move] [to Spain / to Japan / abroad / to a new city].

Vad spännande! Varför just [Spanien / Japan / Italien / Tyskland]?

Wonderful! Why [Spain / Japan / Italy / Germany] in particular?

Jag älskar [maten / kulturen / historien / språket / människorna].

I love [the food / the culture / the history / the language / the people].

Låter bra. Vad vill du göra efter det?

Sounds good. What would you like to do after that?

Kanske [fortsätta studera / lära mig ett nytt språk / börja en ny hobby / bilda familj].

Maybe [continue studying / learn a new language / start a new hobby / start a family].

Verkligen intressant!

Really interesting!

Det var verkligen trevligt att prata med dig.

It was really nice talking with you.

Detsamma! Vi ses snart.

Same here! See you soon.

Hej då!

Bye!

Engine 284: Talking about Emotions

Standard Swedish	Spoken Swedish	English
Hej Tiina, idag är jag glad och nöjd.	Hej Tiina, idag är jag glad och nöjd.	Hi Tiina, today I'm happy and content.
Härligt! Jag har varit trött hela morgonen.	Härligt! Jag har varit trött hela morgonen.	Great! I've been tired all morning.
Varför är du arg?	Varför är du arg?	Why are you angry?
Jag är inte arg, men igår var jag besviken.	Jag är inte arg, men igår var jag besviken.	I'm not angry, but yesterday I was disappointed.
Jag var entusiastisk igår eftersom vädret var vackert.	Jag var entusiastisk igår eftersom vädret var fint.	I was excited yesterday because the weather was beautiful.
Jag däremot var lugn när jag läste en bok.	Jag däremot var lugn när jag läste en bok.	I, on the other hand, was calm while reading a book.
Imorgon vill jag vara glad och avslappnad.	Imorgon vill jag vara glad och avslappnad.	Tomorrow I want to be joyful and relaxed.
Det låter bra! Jag vill vara hoppfull och nyfiken.	Det låter bra! Jag vill vara hoppfull och nyfiken.	That sounds good! I want to be hopeful and curious.
Om det regnar kanske jag är nervös inför resan.	Om det regnar kanske jag är nervös inför resan.	If it rains, I might be nervous about the trip.
Jag lovar att förbli lugn även om det blir åska.	Jag lovar att vara lugn även om det blir åska.	I promise to stay calm, even if there's a thunderstorm.

Engine 285: Descriptions

Standard Swedish	Spoken Swedish	English
Skulle du kunna berätta var du bor, vad du arbetar med och vilka dina fritidsintressen är?	Kan du berätta var du bor, vad du jobbar med och vad du gillar att göra på fritiden?	Could you tell where you live, what you do for work, and what your hobbies are?
Jag bor numera i Berlin i ett livligt område nära Alexanderplatz. Jag arbetar som programmerare på ett stort internationellt företag, och mitt arbete är både utmanande och givande. På min fritid reser jag ofta till Spanien, särskilt till Barcelona, eftersom jag tycker om varma stränder, utsökt mat och en levande kultur. På hösten besöker jag också Frankrike, små soliga kuststäder där atmosfären är lugn och vackert färgstark.	Jag bor nu i Berlin i ett livligt område nära Alexanderplatz. Jag jobbar som programmerare på ett stort internationellt företag, och jobbet är både utmanande och givande. På fritiden reser jag ofta till Spanien, särskilt Barcelona, eftersom jag gillar varma stränder, god mat och en levande kultur. På hösten åker jag också till Frankrike, små soliga kuststäder där det är lugnt och färgstarkt.	I live now in Berlin in a lively area near Alexanderplatz. I work as a programmer in a big international company, and my work is both challenging and rewarding. In my free time, I often travel to Spain, especially Barcelona, because I like warm beaches, delicious food, and vibrant culture. In the fall, I also visit small sunny beach towns in France where the atmosphere is peaceful and beautifully colorful.
Jag bor i Helsingfors i ett lugnt område nära havet och grönskande parker. Jag är lärare och undervisar engelska för gymnasieelever i en modern och ljus skola. På min fritid ägnar jag mig åt fotografering, och jag älskar särskilt höstpromenader vid havet där löven lyser i klart orange och rött. Dessutom dansar jag ofta	Jag bor i Helsingfors i ett lugnt område nära havet och gröna parker. Jag är lärare och undervisar engelska för gymnasieelever i en modern och ljus skola. På fritiden håller jag på med fotografering, och jag älskar särskilt höstpromenader vid havet där löven lyser i starkt orange och rött. Jag dansar också ofta på helgerna	I live in Helsinki in a quiet area near the sea and green parks. I'm a teacher and teach English to high school students in a modern, bright school. In my free time, I do photography, and I especially love autumn walks by the seaside where the leaves shine bright orange and red. I also dance often on weekends with my friends

Standard Swedish	Spoken Swedish	English
på helgerna med mina vänner och besöker ibland små färgglada byar i Italien på sommaren där livet är avslappnat och maten alltid är färsk och god.	med mina vänner och åker ibland till små färgglada byar i Italien på sommaren där livet är lugnt och maten alltid är färsk och god.	and sometimes visit small, colorful villages in Italy in the summer where life is relaxed and the food is always fresh and tasty.

Engine 286: Simple Introductions

Standard Swedish	Spoken Swedish	English
Får jag presentera dig…	Får jag presentera dig…	May I introduce you…
Det här är min vän Matti.	Det här är min kompis Matti.	This is my friend Matti.
Han/Hon är min kollega från jobbet.	Det är min jobbkompis.	He/She is my colleague.
Trevligt att träffas.	Kul att träffas.	Nice to meet you.
Trevligt att äntligen träffas!	Kul att äntligen ses!	Great to finally meet you!
Vad arbetar du med?	Vad jobbar du med?	What do you do for work?
Han/Hon arbetar som lärare.	Han/Hon jobbar som lärare.	He/She works as a teacher.
Han/Hon undervisar i engelska.	Han/Hon lär ut engelska.	He/She teaches English.
Var arbetar du?	Var jobbar du?	Where do you work?
Jag är läkare på ett sjukhus.	Jag är läkare på ett sjukhus.	I'm a doctor at a hospital.

Standard Swedish	Spoken Swedish	English
Jag känner också en läkare.	Jag känner också en läkare.	I also know a doctor.
Är detta din familjemedlem?	Är det här din familjemedlem?	Is this your family member?
Han/Hon är min kusin.	Han/Hon är min kusin.	He/She is my cousin.
Hon är min mamma.	Det är min mamma.	She is my mother.
Han är min man.	Det är min man.	He is my husband.
Tack för introduktionen.	Tack för presentationen.	Thanks for the introduction.
Ha en trevlig kväll allihop!	Ha en trevlig kväll allihop!	Have a nice evening, everyone!
Det var trevligt att träffas.	Det var kul att träffas.	It was a pleasure to meet you.
Vi ses igen snart.	Vi ses snart.	Let's meet again soon.

Engine 287: The Conversation Continues

Du har nått slutet av den här boken.	You have reached the end of this book.
Men samtalet slutar inte här.	But the conversation does not end here.
Varje språk öppnar ett nytt sätt att knyta kontakt,	Every language opens a new way to connect,
att förstå,	to understand,
och att utforska världen.	and to explore the world.
Prova att säga något i ett samtal.	Try something conversational (literally "in conversation").
Försök att prata lite.	Try speaking a little.

Prata lite idag.	Speak a little today.
Prata igen imorgon.	Speak again tomorrow.
Säg något.	Say something.
Säg något på svenska.	Say something in Language.
Och om du vill…	And if you wish…
Säg något på ett nytt språk.	Say something in a new language.
Samtalet fortsätter.	The conversation continues.

Appendix 1: Quick Guide: "en" and "ett" Nouns

Swedish does not mark gender, but many Romance languages do.

Swedish nouns belong to two categories:

- **en-words (common gender)**
- **ett-words (neuter)**

There is no simple rule that works 100% of the time, but clear patterns can help.

Most Nouns Are "en" (~75–80%)

Start here by default.

Common categories:

- **People and professions**
  en person, en lärare, en vän
- **Animals**
  en hund, en katt
- **Most everyday objects**
  en bok (book), en stol (chair), en bil (car)
- **Many abstract ideas**
  en idé, en känsla

If unsure, **"en" is usually the safer guess.**

"ett" Nouns (~20–25%)

Less common, but still important.

Common patterns:

- **Many inanimate objects**
  ett bord (table), ett hus (house)
- **Materials and substances**
  ett vatten (rare in use), ett guld (in certain contexts)
- **Words ending in -eri, -um, -ment**
  ett bageri, ett museum, ett dokument

- **Many one-syllable neutral objects**
  ett glas, ett brev

Adjective agreement (basic pattern) with the nouns

- *en stor bok* (a big book)
- *ett stort hus* (a big house)

Plural forms (often simplified in conversation)

- *stora böcker* (big books)

Important Reality

There are **exceptions**, and "en / ett" must be learned with the word:

- *en stol* (chair)
- *ett bord* (table)

The best strategy:
Learn the noun **with its article** (*en bok*, *ett hus*), not separately.

Usage in This Book

This book introduces **en/ett naturally through conversation patterns**.

You will see nouns repeated in context, allowing patterns to develop through use rather than memorization.

Start with the pattern. Use it. The rest will follow.

What Makes Swedish Easier

- No gender agreement based on the speaker
- No masculine/feminine adjective forms
- Consistent patterns once **en/ett** is learned

Appendix 2: Pronunciation Guide

(Say it out loud — perfection not required)

Swedish pronunciation is **consistent once you learn the patterns**, but unlike Finnish, it is **not always spelled exactly as it sounds.**

Don't worry—you don't need perfection.
You need **clear sounds + rhythm + repetition.**

Quick Explanation for Swedish Using: Du vs Dig / Med dig

Swedish	English	Use
Och du?	And you?	Return same question
Hur är det med dig?	How about you?	General "with you" situation
Och jobbet?	How about work?	Topic shift
Tänk om…	What if…	Suggestion
Och sen?	And then?	Next step
Vad sägs om…	What about…	Reflective idea

Swedish	English
Hur är läget?	How are things going?
Bra. Hur är det med dig?	Good. How about you?
Ganska bra. Jag har mycket att göra. Och du?	Pretty good. I have a lot of work. And you?
Samma här. Ska vi ta en kaffe senare?	Same here. What if we go for coffee later?
Bra idé. Vad sägs om imorgon?	Good idea. What about tomorrow?

---

1. The Big Rule (Good News First)

Swedish is **learnable by listening and repeating.**

What matters most:

- clear vowels
- natural rhythm
- relaxed speech

You do **not** need perfect pronunciation to be understood.

---

2. Vowels (The Most Important Part)

Swedish has **9 vowel letters**, often with **long and short versions**:

Letter	Sounds like	Example	Say it like
A	ah / short a	mat	maht (food)
E	eh / ay	se	seh (see)
I	ee	is	ees (ice)
O	oo / oh	sol	sool (sun)
U	oo (rounded)	hus	hoos (house)
Y	French "u"	ny	lips rounded "ee"
Å	aw	gå	gaw (go)
Ä	eh (cat-like)	här	hehr (here)
Ö	rounded "e"	dörr	deuhr

Long vs Short Vowels

Length **changes meaning**:

- **tak** = tahk (roof)
- **tack** = tahk (thank you, shorter vowel + longer consonant)

Rule of thumb:

- **Single consonant → long vowel**

- **Double consonant → short vowel**

---

3. Consonants (Mostly Familiar)

Most consonants are similar to English, but a few are important:

Letter	Sound
R	Light roll or soft English R
J	Like "y" in *yes*
G	Soft "y" before e, i, y, ä, ö
K	Soft "sh" before e, i, y, ä, ö
SJ sound	Unique Swedish "sh" (sj, stj, sk before soft vowels)

Examples:

- **kyrka** → "shir-ka"
- **sjö** → soft "sh" sound

◆ 4. Stress (Very Important)

Most Swedish words stress the **first syllable**:

- **TA-lar** (speak)
- **SVEN-ska** (Swedish)

If you stress early, you will sound more natural.

---

5. Melody (The Real Secret)

Swedish has a **musical rhythm**.

Think:

- rising and falling tone
- smooth flow
- not flat

This is what makes Swedish sound:
calm
melodic
natural

---

6. Rhythm Tip

Swedish speech is:

smooth · flowing · relaxed

Don't rush.
Let the sentence **breathe.**

---

7. Your Only Job

You do NOT need:

- perfect accent
- perfect tone

You ONLY need:
clear vowels
natural rhythm
willingness to speak

Everything else improves naturally.

---

8. About Sound Changes

Swedish sometimes **changes pronunciation slightly in speech**:

- "det är" → **de e**
- "jag är" → **ja e**

You will **hear this before you understand it.**
That's normal.

---

9. Common Sound Patterns

Soft Consonants (Very Important)

Pattern	Sound
k + e/i/y/ä/ö	"sh"
g + e/i/y/ä/ö	"y"
sk + soft vowel	"sh"

Examples:

- **kemi** → sheh-mi
- **ge** → yeh
- **sked** → shed

---

10. Swedish "Sh" Sounds (Important but Don't Overthink)

Swedish has multiple "sh" sounds:

- **sj** (sjö)
- **sk** (before soft vowels)
- **stj** (stjärna)

You don't need to master this immediately.
Just aim for a **soft "sh" sound.**

Final Reminder

Say it out loud.
Use the engines.
Repeat naturally.

Fluency comes from familiarity.

Closing Line

Säg det högt.
Say it out loud.

Samtalet fortsätter.
The conversation continues.

Appendix 3: Swedish Sound Quick Map

Use this as a **fast visual anchor.**
Don't memorize—**recognize and repeat.**

Core Vowels (Most Important)

Letter	Sound	Tip
A	ah	open mouth
E	eh / ay	short vs long
I	ee	always clear
O	oo / oh	varies slightly
U	oo (rounded)	lips forward
Y	tight "ee" (rounded lips)	like French "u"
Å	aw	like "more"
Ä	eh (cat-like)	relaxed
Ö	rounded "e"	lips forward

Golden Rule:
Vowel length changes meaning

Long vs Short Pattern

Pattern	Result
Vowel + 1 consonant	LONG vowel
Vowel + double consonant	SHORT vowel

Examples:

- **tak** → long vowel

- **tack** → short vowel

Consonant Shortcuts

Pattern	Sound
J	y (yes)
R	light roll
K + e/i/y/ä/ö	sh
G + e/i/y/ä/ö	y
SK + soft vowel	sh

Swedish "Sh" Sound Map

Spelling	Sound
sj	soft "sh"
sk + e/i/y/ä/ö	"sh"
stj	"sh"

Don't overthink—**use one soft "sh" sound**

Stress Rule

Usually first syllable:

- **SVEN-ska**
- **TA-lar**

Melody Rule (Critical)

Swedish = **musical language**

Think:

- rise ↗

- fall ↘
- smooth flow

Rhythm Formula

clear + calm + connected

Your Shortcut to Fluency

You don't need:

- perfect accent
- perfect rules

You need:
repetition
listening
speaking

Appendix 4: Top 20 Swedish Pronunciation Fixes

These are the **real blockers** for learners.

---

1. Flat English Tone

X speaking monotone

O add rise/fall → musical speech

---

2. Ignoring Vowel Length

X mixing long/short

O stretch or shorten clearly

---

3. Saying "Y" like English Y

X yes sound

O rounded “ee” (tight lips)

---

4. Confusing Å, Ä, Ö

X treating them the same

O each has a **distinct sound**

---

5. Over-pronouncing R

X heavy English R

O light tap or soft roll

---

6. Ignoring Double Consonants

X same length

O double = shorter vowel + stronger stop

---

7. Mispronouncing “SJ”

X hard “sh”

O soft, airy “sh”

---

8. Not Softening K/G

X “kemi” = kemi

O “kemi” = shemi

---

9. Speaking Too Fast

X rushed

O slow + clear

---

10. Translating Word-for-Word

X English rhythm

O Swedish rhythm

---

11. Skipping Melody

X flat delivery

O rising + falling tone

---

12. Overthinking Grammar

X hesitation

O speak first, adjust later

---

13. Fear of Mistakes

X silence

O speak anyway

---

14. Ignoring Listening Practice

X reading only

O listen + repeat

---

15. Not Using Patterns

X random sentences

O repeat structures

---

16. Over-articulating Every Letter

X robotic speech

O natural flow

---

17. Not Linking Words

X choppy speech
O connect phrases

---

18. Avoiding Conversation Fillers

X unnatural pauses
O use:

- "ja…"
- "så…"
- "mm…"

---

19. Expecting Perfection

X waiting too long
O speak early

---

20. Not Repeating Enough

X one-time exposure
O repetition builds fluency

◆ Final Coaching Note

Fluency is NOT:

- vocabulary size
- grammar perfection

Fluency IS:

- familiarity
- repetition
- comfort speaking

Final Line (Keep This — It's Strong)

Säg det högt.
Say it out loud.

Samtalet fortsätter.

Core "en / ett" Noun List

EN Words (Common Gender)

People & Roles

- en person — person
- en vän — friend
- en man — man
- en kvinna — woman
- en lärare — teacher
- en student — student
- en chef — boss
- en kollega — colleague

Everyday Objects

- en bok — book
- en stol — chair
- en dörr — door
- en nyckel — key
- en telefon — phone
- en dator — computer
- en väska — bag
- en klocka — clock/watch

Places & Common Things

- en stad — city
- en butik — shop
- en restaurang — restaurant
- en park — park
- en väg — road
- en plats — place

Food & Daily Life

- en kaffe — coffee
- en smörgås — sandwich
- en frukt — fruit
- en måltid — meal

Abstract Concepts

- en idé — idea
- en känsla — feeling
- en plan — plan
- en möjlighet — opportunity
- en fråga — question
- en tid — time

ETT Words (Neuter)

Common Objects

- ett bord — table
- ett hus — house
- ett rum — room
- ett fönster — window

- ett glas — glass
- ett brev — letter

Technology & Modern Life

- ett meddelande — message
- ett konto — account
- ett program — program
- ett system — system

Places & Spaces

- ett hotell — hotel
- ett kontor — office
- ett kök — kitchen

Food & Materials

- ett äpple — apple
- ett bröd — bread
- ett vatten — water *(rare standalone, but useful conceptually)*

Abstract Concepts

- ett problem — problem
- ett svar — answer
- ett sätt — way
- ett liv — life
- ett beslut — decision

How to Use This List (Engine Integration)

Always practice as:

- **en bok → boken → böcker**
- **ett hus → huset → hus**

Build patterns:

- *Jag har en bok.*
- *Jag ser ett hus.*
- *Det är ett problem.*

Key Learning Insight

- ~75–80% of nouns = **en**
- ~20–25% = **ett**

So:
Default to "en" → confirm with exposure → reinforce through use

---

Author's Intent

Swedish with Purpose
Come Play. In Swedish.

Swedish Conversation Begins with Purpose
Fluency grows through familiarity, not speed.

Natural acquisition works.
It has worked for millennia.
The question is not if it works —
the question is how to **accelerate it intentionally**.

The result is not artificial speed.
It is **structured familiarity**.

Children learn to speak a language long before they study grammar. They acquire language through curiosity, repetition, safety, and meaningful interaction. Only later do they learn the rules that explain what they are already able to say.

Language develops through interacting processes:

- **Acquisition** — natural, subconscious absorption through meaningful exposure

- **Language Study** — conscious understanding of grammar and structure
- **Repetition** — frequent, daily use in natural and engaging contexts

Language acquisition increases when we are:

- **Curious** — dialogue, interests, scenes, personal meaning
- **Interested** — adventure, storytelling, descriptions, outcomes
- **Relaxed and Safe** — imagination and play lower mental resistance
- **Exposed Frequently** — speaking, listening, reading, and writing regularly

When stress rises, learning tends to stall:

- **Embarrassment** → focus shifts to correctness
- **Fear of mistakes** → following rules replace communication
- **Anxiety** → mistake-free thinking replaces understanding
- **Pressure** → focus on immediate correctness

The goal of this book is to keep us in the **slight stretch zone**:

- **Too easy** → no progress
- **Slight stretch** → acquisition
- **Frustration** → maybe progress or quitting
- **Too hard** → confusion

Swedish with Purpose combines:

- Dialogs that sparks curiosity - "slight stretch" zone
- Dual directional bilingual engines
- Pattern recognition through conversation

Learning thrives in environments that feel curious, engaging and inviting.

**If this book helps you say even one sentence in Swedish,
the conversation has already begun.**

About the Author

Mark Anderson, PhD writes at the intersection of science, language, regulatory systems, and artificial intelligence. His work explores how intelligence emerges across disciplines, while his language-learning books focus on making patterns clear, usable, and enjoyable.

He began developing these conversation engines after noticing that many language books offered either very basic phrases or dense grammar explanations, but few natural conversations people could actually use. *Swedish with Purpose* was created to help fill that gap.

If you open this book and say even one word in Swedish, the experiment has already worked.

Samtalet fortsätter. | The conversation continues.

Back Cover

Swedish with Purpose: *Come Play. In Swedish.*

Practice with purpose.

Work through the conversation engines aloud — with repetition, focus, and intention — and something begins to change.

Conversation no longer feels distant. It becomes usable.

With consistent practice, we can build toward A1 to B1-level speaking, move into B2 in everyday situations, and even stretch toward C1-level performance in more demanding conversational tasks.

More importantly, this conversation approach builds something deeper: confidence, responsiveness, and the ability to think and speak in the moment.

Because when we practice with purpose, we do more than memorize words — we begin to think, respond, and take part in real conversation in Swedish.

It's a **conversational operating system**. You practice **one thing — on purpose.**

Talk with a friend — or your favorite coffee cup.

If this book helps you say **even one sentence in Swedish**,
the conversation has already begun.

Säg något på svenska. | Say Something in Swedish.
Kom och lek. På svenska. | Come play. In Swedish.

Description

Swedish with Purpose is designed for learners who want to start speaking Swedish sooner — without rushing, memorizing endless vocabulary lists, or waiting to feel "ready."

Built on familiarity rather than speed, this book gives you small, repeatable ways to say something meaningful in Swedish from the very beginning.

Instead of overwhelming you with complex grammar rules, it introduces a focused system of reusable conversation patterns called conversation engines.

Each engine models a short, realistic exchange — giving you something concrete to say immediately.

Through repetition, variation, and gradual expansion, your ability to respond begins to grow naturally.

Inside the book:

- Over 280 structured conversation engines
- Real-life topics: daily life, travel, food, health, work, and more
- Advanced scenarios: professional communication, negotiation, and social interaction
- Side-by-side Swedish–English format
- Flexible use: start in either language and respond in the other

This is not about speaking fast.
It's about speaking with purpose.

Start anywhere.
Say something in Swedish.

How the Engines were designed

Layer	Engines	Capability	What Changes
Basic	1–40	Survival Conversation	You can respond, ask simple questions, coffee, and participate
Functional	41–77	Daily Life	You can handle common situations (a memory, learning, a habit, like the look of something)
Expressive	78–120	Emotions & Opinions	You can describe feelings, preferences, reactions
Reflective	121–160	Identity & Memory	You can talk about your life, past, and experiences
Philosophical	161–200	Meaning & Perspective	You can discuss ideas, beliefs, frustration, and abstract topics
Meta-Conversation	201–240	Control & Repair	Nouns, verbs, daily news, doctor, police, where you can guide, fix, and manage conversations

Layer	Engines	Capability	What Changes
Conversation Integration	241–287	Natural Flow	Gas station, hospital visit, car accident, conversational words, Flea Circus, personal descriptions, and you combine everything into real, fluid conversation

---

CEFR Note:

Some engines are suitable for beginners **A1–A2**, while others introduce vocabulary and conversational structures often seen in **B1–B2 Swedish**, with occasional sentence patterns approaching **C1-level complexity**.

Consider how we use conversation as:

- *everyday small talk (A1–A2)*
- *personal reflection (B1)*
- *emotional intelligence (B2)*
- *nuanced philosophical/ social insight to career(C1 to C2)*

You decide. You are encouraged to explore and enjoy the language without worrying about level boundaries.Engines help us and AI articulate **values, interpersonal warmth, emotional intelligence, and social perception**, all essential for conversations.

Some engines help develop reflective thinking, our meta-language about communication, emotional awareness, and self-insight. These are key skills for **B2 to early C1** fluency and for training AI to understand conversational strengths.

Perspectives:

Engines are intended to mirror a workplace, school, café, a friendly-group chat, small talk on Thursdays, Fridays, or anytime someone wants to build rapport.

Recognizing conversational patterns is powerful. The goal is active language use, practice and familiarity, and encouraging fluency.

Our daily conversations flow through thoughtful, cognitive-emotional engines that encourages ***memory, reflection, wisdom, and narrative skill****: reflective vocabulary, emotional honesty, storytelling skill, and supportive closure.*

Thinking of conversation as engines, helps us express ***intentions, plans, goals, priorities, time frames, and personal development****.*

Practice strengthens us in our new language ***identity, skills, pride, vocabulary, descriptive fluency, cultural storytelling, values, discussion, and warm social connection****.*

Repetition strengthens our habits, vocabulary, intentionality, behavioral planning, motivational language, and personal development expression.

Use the future tense for discussing hopes and dreams, vision-setting, personal meaning, and gentle interpersonal dialogue.

Reflecting on your life-story expands fluency, reflective vocabulary, past-tense structure, value-based reasoning, emotional insight, and narrative clarity.

Testing conditional language skills builds our new identity so we can explore reasoning, a different personal identity, assess values, and creative introspection.

Small words help keep conversation flowing. Use them to react, think, agree, or show interest.

Some phrases form the foundation of daily conversation. Use them to greet people, ask simple questions, and keep interactions natural.

Engines encourage strong CEFR behavior that prepares us for meaningful long-term conversations and for building or designing AI responses. This is especially important for our B1→C1 mastery.

Speak them aloud.
Use them often.
It also strengthens AI's ability to map how humans perceive each other.
It's subtle, light, and socially fun.

Also by Mark Anderson

- *Tommi the Green Tomato (Bilingual Series)*
- *The Alignment Echo (Books I, II & III) - SciFi*
- *The Accidental Genius & Snackcidents (Cookbook)*
- *Cooking & Cancer - Cooking for someone special (Cookbook)*
- *Does AI Scare You? Yes. No. Maybe. - Artificial Intelligence & Technology*
- *Finnish with Purpose*
- *Portuguese with Purpose - Coming Soon*
- *The Meridian Series: Where time is not fixed—and neither is choice.*
    - *Book 1: The Meridian Paris Protocol - The system is discovered.*
    - *Book 2: The London Recurrence - The system resists control. Coming Soon*
    - *Book 3: The Tokyo Convergence - The system becomes something else.*

Selected References

The following works were helpful in keeping languages grounded, accurate, and naturally focused. They are not required reading, but curious readers are encouraged to explore whenever possible. You choose.

Dictionary

Prismas Engelska Ordbok: Engelsk-Svensk / Svensk-Engelsk. Stockholm: Norstedts Akademiska Förlag, 2018. ISBN-13: 978-9113086588.

Grammar

Holmes, Philip, and Ian Hinchliffe. *Swedish: A Comprehensive Grammar*. 3rd ed. London: Routledge, 2013. ISBN-13: 978-0415584838.

Holmes, Philip, and Ian Hinchliffe. *Swedish: An Essential Grammar*. 2nd ed. London: Routledge, 2003. ISBN-13: 978-0415278850.

Language Acquisition & Use

Krashen, Stephen D. *Principles and Practice in Second Language Acquisition.* Pergamon Press, 1982. ISBN-13: 978-0137100477

Nation, I. S. P. *Learning Vocabulary in Another Language* (2nd ed.). Cambridge University Press, 2013. ISBN-13: 978-1107623026.

Long, Michael H. *Second Language Acquisition and Task-Based Language Teaching.* Wiley-Blackwell, 2015. ISBN-13: Hardcover: 978-0470658932 or Paperback: 978-0470658949.

Cognitive Science & Learning

Kahneman, Daniel. *Thinking, Fast and Slow.* Farrar, Straus and Giroux, 2011. ISBN-13: 978-0374533557.

Dehaene, Stanislas. *How We Learn: Why Brains Learn Better Than Any Machine… for Now.* Viking, 2020. ISBN-13: 978-0525559887.

Reinforcement Learning & Feedback Sutton, Richard S., and Andrew G. Barto. *Reinforcement Learning: An Introduction* (2nd ed.). MIT Press, 2018. ISBN-13: 978-0262039246.

Spoken and Written Language Ong, Walter J. *Orality and Literacy: The Technologizing of the Word.* Routledge, 1982 (reissued editions available). ISBN-13: 978-0415538381.

Image Note:

Artwork was generated with artificial intelligence as a tool. The front cover image depicts Stockholm at blue hour, Sweden. The back cover image is of a generated Swedish Darla horse. Any resemblance to actual scenes is coincidental.

www.ingramcontent.com/pod-product-compliance
Lightning Source LLC
LaVergne TN
LVHW010644110826
845149LV00014B/2948